Wanderlust Unleashed

Wanderlust Unleashed

A Guide to Adventurous Travel

B. Vincent

QuantumQuill Press

CONTENTS

1. Chapter 1: Embracing the Spirit of Adventure — 1
2. Chapter 2: Planning for Adventure — 6
3. Chapter 3: Exploring Remote Destinations — 13
4. Chapter 4: Thrilling Outdoor Activities — 20
5. Chapter 5: Immersing in Cultural Experiences — 28
6. Chapter 6: Documenting Adventures — 35
7. Chapter 7: Overcoming Challenges and Adversity — 44
8. Chapter 8: Sustainable and Responsible Travel Practices — 53
9. Chapter 9: Reflecting on Transformative Experiences — 61
10. Chapter 10: Continuing the Adventure — 69

Copyright © 2024 by B. Vincent

All rights reserved. No part of this book may be reproduced in any manner whatsoever without written permission except in the case of brief quotations embodied in critical articles and reviews.

First Printing, 2024

1

Chapter 1: Embracing the Spirit of Adventure

Grasping the Charm of Daring Travel

Setting out on a bold excursion is something beyond visiting new spots; it's a mission to open the secrets of the world and find the profundities of one's spirit. The appeal of courageous travel lies in the commitment to elating encounters, significant associations, and extraordinary minutes that anticipate past the recognizable. It's tied in with getting out of safe places and embracing the obscure with great enthusiasm, realizing that each experience will leave a permanent imprint on the voyager's heart and psyche. Understanding this charm is an epic and vital move toward embracing the soul of experience and leaving on an excursion.

Defeating fears and reservations

Chasing experience: It is normal to experience fears and reservations that might keep us from completely embracing the unexplored world. Whether it's the feeling of dread toward the unknown, worries about wellbeing, or questions about our own capacities, these hindrances can appear to be impossible now and again. Nonetheless, genuine explorers comprehend that development lies on the opposite side of dread.

Beating these feelings of dread and reservations requires an eagerness to defy them head-on, to recognize their presence without permitting them to direct our activities. It's tied in with perceiving that uneasiness is often an indication of development and propelling ourselves past our apparent restrictions. By making little strides outside our usual ranges of familiarity and progressively extending our limits, we can fabricate the strength and certainty expected to set out on even the most trying experiences.

Through thoughtfulness and self-reflection, we can distinguish the underlying drivers of our feelings of dread and work towards defeating them. Whether through reflection, representation methods, or looking for help from companions and coaches, there are endless procedures for tending to and moderating our tensions.

Eventually, it's memorable and critical that dread is a characteristic piece of the human experience, and it's OK to feel worried while venturing into the unexplored world. What makes the biggest difference is our ability to recognize these feelings of trepidation, face them with fortitude, and keep pushing ahead in spite of them. In doing so, we free ourselves up to a universe of vast potential outcomes and boundless experiences.

Developing a mentality of investigation

At the core of courageous travel lies a mentality of investigation—an unquenchable interest and a hunger for revelation that drives us to search out new encounters and push the limits of our usual ranges of familiarity. Developing this mentality is fundamental to embracing the soul of experience and completely submerging ourselves in the excursion ahead.

To develop an outlook for investigation, we should initially develop a feeling of transparency and interest in our general surroundings. Rather than moving toward new circumstances with fear or doubt, we approach them with a feeling of miracle and fervor, anxious to uncover the unlikely treasures and untold stories that lie just beyond the great beyond.

This mentality of investigation likewise requires an eagerness to embrace the obscure and adjust to surprising difficulties enroute. As opposed to gripping to inflexible plans or assumptions of how our undertakings ought to unfold, we stay adaptable and liberal, permitting ourselves to be directed by instinct and luck.

Moreover, developing a mentality of investigation includes embracing a development-situated viewpoint, seeing misfortunes and deterrents not as disappointments but rather as any open doors for learning and self-awareness. Rather than being deterred by misfortunes, we approach them with flexibility and assurance, perceiving that each challenge we conquer carries us one bit closer to our objectives.

Eventually, developing an outlook of investigation is tied in with embracing the excursion as much as the objective, tracking down bliss and satisfaction during the time spent on disclosure and self-revelation. By cultivating a feeling of interest, receptiveness, and flexibility, we can leave our experiences with a feeling of direction and energy, prepared to embrace anything that the street ahead may bring.

Embracing Immediacy and Unusualness

One of the most invigorating parts of brave travel is the component of suddenness and eccentricity that accompanies investigating the unexplored world. Embracing this suddenness is fundamental for opening the maximum capacity of our experiences and permitting ourselves to drench right now completely.

In a world that frequently feels overbooked and unsurprising, embracing immediacy can be a freeing experience. It permits us to break liberated from the requirements of routine and assumption, freeing ourselves up to surprising open doors and fortunate experiences that can enhance our movements in manners we won't ever envision.

Embracing immediacy likewise requires a readiness to relinquish control and give up on the progression of the excursion. Rather than carefully arranging everything about our undertakings, we permit ourselves to be directed by instinct and intuition, believing that the universe will give us precisely what we want, precisely when we want it.

Obviously, embracing suddenness doesn't mean pulling out all the stops altogether. Finding some kind of harmony between embracing the obscure and avoiding potential risks to guarantee our security and prosperity is significant. By staying aware of our environmental elements and listening to our instincts, we can explore the erratic, exciting bends in the road of our undertakings effortlessly.

Eventually, embracing suddenness is tied in with embracing life in the entirety of its untidy, unusual brilliance. It's tied in with expressing yes to the unforeseen, quickly jumping all over chances as they emerge, and permitting ourselves to be completely present in every second. In doing so, we free ourselves up to a universe of limitless potential outcomes and vast undertakings that are not far off.

Setting Sensible Assumptions for Courageous Excursions

While the charm of daring travel might summon pictures of epic scenes and adrenaline-energized ventures, moving toward our excursions with a feeling of authenticity and practicality is fundamental. Setting practical assumptions not only guarantees a more charming and satisfying experience but also assists us with exploring the unavoidable difficulties and vulnerabilities that accompany investigating the unexplored world.

Setting reasonable assumptions starts with careful exploration and acquiring an unmistakable comprehension of the objections we intend to raise. This includes finding out about the nearby culture, environment, and customs, as well as any possible dangers or difficulties we might experience enroute. By equipping ourselves with information and data, we can all the more likely plan for the real factors of our undertakings and stay away from any upsetting astonishments.

It's likewise vital to evaluate our own physical and close-to-home limits and design our experiences. While it's normal to need to propel ourselves out of our usual ranges of familiarity, it's similarly critical to know our own limits and pay attention to our bodies and psyches when they signal the requirement for rest or unwinding. By finding a steady speed and focusing on taking care of ourselves, we can guarantee that our undertakings are manageable and charming over the long haul.

Moreover, setting reasonable assumptions includes embracing the startling and staying adaptable even with change. In spite of our best-laid plans, things may not generally go as per plan, and that is fine. By moving toward our undertakings with a receptive outlook and an eagerness to adjust to unexpected conditions, we can change even the most difficult circumstances into significant opportunities for growth and loved recollections.

Finally, setting reasonable assumptions is tied in with tracking down a harmony among desire and common sense, experience and security, fervor and care. By moving toward our excursions with modesty, regard, and a solid portion of idealism, we can leave our experiences with certainty, realizing that we are good to go for anything that the street ahead may bring.

2

Chapter 2: Planning for Adventure

Investigating Off-the-Beach Destinations

When embarking on an expedition, one frequently deviates from the conventional tourist routes in order to investigate destinations that are not conventional. Conducting research on such unusual locations is an essential initial course of action when organizing an unforgettable journey.

By conducting an extensive review of travel literature, online forums, and firsthand testimonies from fellow explorers, one can potentially discover lesser-known treasures and jewels that are not easily accessible. Unknown destinations, such as a secluded mountain village situated in the midst of the wilderness or a remote island sanctuary devoid of mass tourism, present the potential for exploration of untamed beauty and genuine experiences.

When conducting research on unusual travel destinations, it is critical to take into account various aspects, including cultural sensitivity, safety, and accessibility. Although certain remote areas may demand comprehensive travel arrangements and logistical forethought, others may present obstacles such as linguistic barriers or indigenous customs. By tenaciously endeavoring through thorough examination and storing up an abundance of data, we can ensure that our undertakings come to pass effortlessly.

Besides, by leading examinations on less popular objections, we can add to the economic value of the travel industry drives and backing neighborhood networks. By choosing to visit less notable objections, we can add to the relief of the unfavorable impacts of the over-the-travel industry on prestigious vacation spots and convey monetary benefits to additional confined locales that need help. Fundamentally, investigating off-the-beaten-path destinations entails imbibing the spirit of exploration and adventure in its most authentic form. Through venturing beyond our established boundaries and investigating lesser-traveled paths, we grant ourselves access to an inexhaustible realm of potentialities and indelible encounters that lie beyond the threshold.

Allocating Funds for Voluntary Travel Experiences

Commencing an audacious expedition necessitates meticulous financial strategizing to guarantee complete immersion in the forthcoming experiences without the weight of financial strain. Budgeting for adventurous travel experiences necessitates the inclusion of supplementary expenditures that may transpire during the journey, in addition to the estimation of transportation, lodging, and activity costs.

Prior to all else, it is critical to determine a practical travel budget in consideration of our personal financial situations and travel inclinations. This necessitates considering variables including the intended itinerary, the intended stops, and the preferred standard of opulence and comfort. By establishing explicit financial limits at the outset, we can prevent unnecessary expenditures and guarantee that our journeys remain feasible.

Apart from essential expenditures like lodging and transportation, it is critical to allocate funds for luxuries such as activities, meals, and mementos. Although certain thrilling endeavors may entail a substantial financial investment, those who are willing to look for them will frequently discover more affordable alternatives. There are numerous strategies that can be employed to reduce travel expenses while maintaining the quality of the experience. For instance, one could substitute upscale restaurants for nightly street cuisine or resort accommodations.

Additionally, to prepare a financial plan for audacious travel encounters, it is important to represent unanticipated consumption and crises that could unfold all through the journey. This involves distributing assets to a possibility reserve, fully expecting unexpected occasions like health-related crises, postponements in transportation, or unforeseen changes to our schedule. By making vital monetary arrangements, we can leave on our excursions with confirmation that we are satisfactorily prepared to face any unanticipated deterrents that might emerge.

Planning for bold travel encounters eventually requires achieving an amicable harmony between financial judiciousness and the journey for permanent encounters. Through meticulous budgeting and planning, we can confidently commence our travel endeavors, secure in the knowledge that we possess the necessary financial means to wholeheartedly appreciate the voyage that lies ahead.

Packing Essentials for Unpredictable Conditions and Rugged Terrains

In order to embark on an exciting journey, it is necessary to prepare sensibly, guaranteeing that we possess every essential item required to traverse difficult terrain and unforeseeable circumstances with confidence and ease. Every objective, from distant wilderness woodlands to far-off mountain trails, presents its own interesting difficulties; consequently, bringing the proper hardware can essentially add to the confirmation of a solid and pleasurable undertaking.

It is vital to buy strong, lightweight, and flexible outside hardware of predominant quality that can endure the afflictions of gutsy travel. The bundle comprises dampness-wicking clothing that is fitting for layering, strong climbing footwear that offers uncommon lower leg support, and a tough rucksack that gives adequate compartment space to everyday necessities like water, bites, and emergency treatment supplies.

Pressing fundamentals for rough territory and eccentric circumstances incorporates, as well as attire and footwear, endurance supplies, crisis sanctuary, and route instruments. Arrangements, for example, a trustworthy tent and hiking bed for nighttime setting up camp and a reliable guide and compass for crossing unknown paths, are basic for shielding our government assistance and guaranteeing our wellbeing in nature.

Also, it is important to consider different parts of the objective's environment and territory while choosing our assets, including temperature variances, precipitation, and landscape highlights. This may encompass bringing along waterproof equipment for destinations with precipitation, sun protection for humid and sunny climates, and insect repellent for regions susceptible to mosquitoes and other pests.

At last, while getting the fundamentals for brave travel, it is urgent to consider the ecological effect of our gear determinations and bend over backward to decrease our carbon footprint. This might involve choosing naturally great and supportable items, bringing reusable utensils and water containers, and diminishing the utilization of single-use plastics and bundling.

Through wise and obliging pressing, we can ensure that we are totally equipped to go up against any obstructions and ventures that might emerge during our journey. Furnished with the appropriate gear, we can unhesitatingly and safely embrace our undertakings, for example, navigating unavailable pathways and persevering through brutal circumstances.

Crisis Readiness and Wellbeing Safety Measures

Although daring travel offers exciting encounters and permanent memories, it is important to put wellbeing first and stay prepared for unexpected crises that might happen during the excursion. By carrying out deterrent measures to protect our physical and emotional wellness, we can earnestly take part in the experience without unjustifiable concern or trouble.

It is absolutely critical that we conduct a broad examination of the expected risks and dangers related to our chosen objective, like height ailments, cataclysmic events, and natural life experiences. Armed with this comprehension, we can limit our openness to risk and, whenever the situation allows, stay away from unsafe circumstances by playing it safe.

Wellbeing insurance and crisis readiness incorporate examination as well as the execution of commonsense measures to ease possible risks and dangers. Possible things to be brought along may comprise specialized gadgets like an individual finder guide or satellite telephone, as well as medical aid packs and crisis covers. Route, cover development, and fire making are a couple of the key wild basic instincts that should be dominated. Additionally, the ability to administer first aid in an emergency is crucial.

Moreover, maintaining communication and remaining well-informed are critical elements of emergency preparedness and safety protocols. This process may entail enrolling with local governmental bodies or embassy services, informing reliable acquaintances or relatives of our travel plans, and remaining informed about the latest weather predictions and travel advisories pertaining to our intended location.

A final piece of advice is to exercise caution and rely on our instincts when confronted with unfamiliar or potentially hazardous situations. Ensuring safety should invariably take precedence over all else, including discouraging hazardous activities and seeking aid from local authorities or fellow travelers.

By adopting preventive strategies to guarantee our personal security and welfare, we can confidently commence our expeditions, cognizant of the fact that we are equipped to confront any obstacles that may arise. Although it is impossible to foretell or avert all emergencies, being well-prepared provides the assurance that we can wholeheartedly embrace the experience and maximize our daring journeys.

Exploring Unusual Lodging and Transportation Alternatives

A pleasure inherent in adventurous travel is the chance to venture beyond our comfort zones and fully engage in one-of-a-kind and indelible experiences, both while traveling and in our makeshift residences. Investigating unconventional methods of transportation and resting under the stars in far-off wild campgrounds are two instances of how looking through unmistakable facilities and transportation choices improves the validity and fervor of our campaigns.

In the domain of housing, bold voyagers are given a broad determination, enveloping traditional motels and store lodgings as well as additional abnormal options like treehouses, yurts, and eco-lodges detached inside the wild. These distinctive lodgings provide not only a place to recharge our exhausted bodies but also a significant opportunity to engage with the surrounding environment and culture.

Beyond lodging, adventurous travel provides access to an array of non-traditional modes of conveyance that enable us to investigate our destination in manners that are equally as memorable as the expedition itself. Engaging in alternative modes of transportation, such as traversing remote waterways by kayak or canoe, embarking on a multi-day trek through rugged terrain, or navigating winding mountain roads on a motorcycle or bicycle, provides individuals with a more profound connection to the environment and an enhanced sense of autonomy and self-reliance.

By selecting atypical lodgings and modes of transportation, we can additionally contribute to the advancement of sustainable tourism endeavors and local communities, given that a significant number of these unconventional options are owned and operated by enthusiastic locals eager to impart their culture and heritage to tourists. Our selection of accommodations at locally-owned guesthouses and participation in tours operated by environmentalists can effect positive change in the communities we visit and establish an enduring heritage of conscientious travel.

In the end, the pursuit of distinctive lodging and transportation alternatives signifies an embrace of the spirit of exploration and a willingness to confront novel and unforeseen encounters. Unusual travel experiences, such as supogenously lodging in a converted train carriage situated in a desolate desert or caching a transport on a fishing vessel to a secluded island paradise, inspire us to continue our worldly exploration with receptive hearts and minds.

3

Chapter 3: Exploring Remote Destinations

Investigating the Untamed Wild by means of Journeying

Untainted wild journeying addresses the zenith of thinking for even a moment to travel, giving a remarkable chance to draw in with the perfect, pure wonder of the climate profoundly. Traveling through imposing mountain ranges, thick wilderness backwoods, or extensive parched scenes, wild trips give gutsy people an unmatched chance to restore an association with the intrinsic rhythms of the regular world and experience an unrivaled feeling of freedom and elation.

The allure of undertaking endeavors through strange wildlives in the trouble and advantage of crossing confined and habitually cruel scenes, where each advance yields new experiences and unanticipated experiences. The excursion will go through remarkable scenes, including stowed-away valleys, immaculate lakes, transcending tops, and flowing cascades; they will fill you with wonder and modesty despite the brilliance of nature.

Besides, endeavoring in the strange wild gives people a valuable chance to challenge themselves and adventure beyond their usual ranges of familiarity as they go up against impressive plummets, risky trips, and an impulsive climate. The endeavor involves a journey of reflection and individual turns of events, during which perseverance and assurance are compensated with stunning scenes and examples of the most profound fellowship with the regular habitat.

Notwithstanding, the open door to reconnect with the world's cycles and disengage from the interruptions of present-day life might be the most compensating part of traveling across the untamed wild. Ventilating past the clamoring metropolitan climate, valiant people look for shelter in the quietness of the wild, where the only hearable upgrades comprise far-off natural life calls, the stirring of foliage, and the whirlwind.

Journeying across untamed wilderness is, at its center, a profoundly sustaining, truly burdening, and substantial testing experience that incites significant internal change. This campaign dives into an unknown domain, where every ever-evolving measure brings us closer to the central idea of our credible selves and the boundless quality of the climate.

Managing Isolated Trails and Difficult Terrains

A key part of trying endeavors, crossing blocked-off pathways and troublesome territories furnishes valiant pilgrims with the opportunity to scrutinize their solidarity in probably the most unfriendly and pristine environmental elements on the globe. Unpleasant landscapes, going from bone-chilling tundra and thick timberlands to transcending mountain tops and parched deserts, all charm explorers with the commitment of disclosure and experience, empowering them to set out on a journey of self-revelation.

One can't resist the urge to be enthralled by the feeling of independence and freedom that goes with crossing neglected locales through far-off pathways. Venturers find themselves uncontrolled in the wild, encompassed by confinement and harmony, where each unexpected turn of the path presents new obstructions and unanticipated advantages.

Be that as it may, crossing remote paths isn't without any trace of obstruction. Remote scenes require the utilization of both physical and mental strength because of their deceptive stream intersections, steep grades, and serious weather patterns. It is a preliminary of determination and mastery, where overcoming every hindrance induces a sensation of satisfaction and self-strengthening.

Moreover, traversing remote pathways provides explorers with an opportunity to develop a profound and meaningful connection with the natural world. During their expeditions through remote wilderness and ancient forests, individuals develop an enhanced sense of admiration for the planet's splendor and variety, establishing an enduring and profound connection with the terrain they explore.

However, what could arguably be the most valuable benefit of traversing remote trails is the sense of companionship and collective knowledge gained from undertaking this ordeal with other intrepid individuals. When out hiking with family, friends, or fellow travelers who share similar interests, the connections formed during the journey are just as lasting as the recollections formed.

Fundamentally, traversing remote trails and treacherous terrains entails an expedition of inquiry and maturation, wherein each progressive stride yields fresh perceptions and epiphanies. This serves as evidence of the unwavering determination of the human race and the timeless appeal of the natural world, motivating daring explorers to surpass their boundaries and wholeheartedly embrace uncharted territories.

Exploring Unknown Gems Away from the Tourist Route

Achieving access to lesser-known destinations that are brimming with allure, genuineness, and unexplored splendor is the essence of adventurous travel—discovering hidden treasures off the tourist map. Situated at a distance from densely populated tourist destinations and traveled routes, these obscure treasures await the exploration of daring explorers who are prepared to venture beyond the norm in pursuit of extraordinary and indelible encounters.

The appeal of uncovering obscure treasures resides in the thrill and expectation that accompany venturing into unexplored domains. Each unexpected discovery elicits a mixture of awe and excitement as it transports travelers to a realm unaffected by commercialization and mass tourism. This is valid whether they experience a secret cascade, a separated coastline, or a town that goes back hundreds of years.

Be that as it may, revealing secret gems is about more than just finding unexpected fortunes; it is likewise about laying out a veritable and significant association with the neighborhood culture and local area. As people venture close by the most common way to go in these off-in-an unexpected direction regions, they gain a more significant understanding and deference for the unmistakable individuals, customs, and customs that add to the uniqueness of each spot.

Further, uncovering less popular objections gives courageous people a valuable chance to disengage from the mass of guests and experience the serenity and segregation of more unfamiliar courses. While crossing quiet towns, journeying across flawless wild, or exploring old vestiges, voyagers look for comfort in the serenity and magnificence of these remote and neglected conditions.

Nonetheless, the greatest advantage of uncovering dark fortunes might be the significant feeling of satisfaction and happiness that goes with the revelation of something really remarkable and particular. Every unanticipated discovery, such as encountering a concealed vantage point offering expansive panoramas or stumbling upon an obscure café specializing in the finest regional gastronomy, transforms into a treasured recollection, showcasing the gratification that can be derived from venturing out on an expedition.

Fundamentally, uncovering lesser-known treasures off the beaten path entails an expedition of investigation and revelation, wherein each detour unveils fresh enticements and pleasures. This assertion highlights the idea that there are various wonders anticipating disclosure on the planet and that the certifiable soul of traveling dwells in embracing the new and finding the uncommon in the commonplace.

Interacting with Local Communities and Indigenous Cultures

Active participation in indigenous cultures and local communities is a fundamental aspect of daring travel, providing visitors with the chance to establish connections with individuals whose way of life has largely persisted throughout the centuries. Located in secluded areas away from commercialized attractions and tourist hoards, these interactions offer a unique and genuine opportunity to gain insight into the diverse and intricate fabric of human existence. They promote empathy, comprehension, and mutual regard between travelers and the communities they visit.

The appeal of actively participating in interactions with indigenous cultures resides in the prospect of acquiring knowledge and understanding from individuals whose customs, beliefs, and practices have persisted for generations; doing so provides a distinctive vantage point from which to survey the world. Engaging in artisanal crafts, participating in traditional ceremonies, or dining with local families are all immersive experiences that provide valuable insights into an enduring and primordial way of life.

However, active participation in indigenous cultures encompasses more than mere acquisition of knowledge; it also involves establishing substantial relationships and fostering comprehension among diverse cultures and lifestyles. By engaging in activities such as sharing stories that have been handed down through generations, breaking bread together as an act of hospitality and camaraderie, and laughing and conversing with newly made friends, travelers discover a humanity that transcends linguistic and cultural boundaries.

Furthermore, active participation in interactions with indigenous cultures provides tourists with an opportunity to aid in the conservation and commemoration of traditional wisdom and heritage. Through the help of neighborhood craftsmen, dynamic cooperation in social celebrations, and respect for hallowed locales and customs, explorers can contribute to the safeguarding of these precious practices for people in the future.

Notwithstanding, the most significant advantage of effectively participating in native societies might be the foundation of enduring kinships and associations. Engaging in experiences such as partaking in a communal meal with indigenous people or seeking the counsel of tribal elders while dancing beneath the stars at a traditional festival—these interactions profoundly impact the intellectual and emotional well-being of travelers, expanding their perspectives and enhancing their lives in unprecedented ways.

Fundamentally, active involvement with indigenous cultures and local communities entails an expedition of enlightenment and rapport, during which each encounter imparts fresh perspectives and disclosures. It serves as a reminder that, in spite of our variations, we are all members of the same human family, united solely by our shared humanity and our mutual curiosity and aspiration to comprehend the world.

Discovering Peace and Isolation in Remote Areas

Discovering peace and quietness in isolated areas is a fundamental aspect of daring journeying, providing tranquility-seekers with the chance to reestablish a connection with the pristine natural environment. Located beyond the disturbances and excesses of the metropolitan environment, these secluded areas provide a haven for the spirit, where individuals can discover tranquility, insight, and a profound sense of equilibrium amidst the splendor and grandeur of unspoiled wilderness.

The appeal of discovering solitude and tranquility resides in the ability to detach oneself from the pressures and obligations of daily existence and fully engage with the natural world. Engaging in activities such as stargazing while camping, strolling along secluded footpaths, or simply meditating by a mountain stream provides opportunities for solitude that afford the chance to restore inner peace, spiritual well-being, and spiritual vigor.

In any case, achieving isolation and serenity requires more than basically sidestepping the clamor and turmoil of the contemporary world; it likewise involves earnestly embracing the magnificence and sensational characteristics of the normal world completely. While wandering into distant regions and observing the amazing quality of transcending mountains, unblemished lakes, and verdant woods, explorers are enlivened by the tirelessness and magnificence of the regular world and lowered by the extent of the planet.

Besides, the chance to find isolation and serenity in distant areas gives explorers the resources to cultivate a more significant sense of identity, mindfulness, and association with the climate. They find space to think, reflect, and reconnect with their deepest contemplations and feelings in the wild, in this way acquiring lucidity and knowledge for their own lives and the world at large.

In any case, maybe the main advantage of finding isolation and serenity is the sensation of restoration and recharging that results from being completely fascinated by the helpful capacities of the normal world. Attributable to the unblemished mountain air, the stirring of leaves in the breeze, or the quieting sound of waves running into the shore, these confined minutes give an amazing chance to revive and reestablish the physical, mental, and otherworldly parts of the voyager. Subsequently, they leave their process feeling fortified, recharged, and ready to face the approaching difficulties and experiences.

Generally, the quest for isolation and serenity in distant regions involves an undertaking of self-investigation and revival, during which every moment spent drenched in the normal world confers new points of view and disclosures. It fills in as a piercing update that amidst the world's problems and unusualness, there exists an unseen safe haven —a domain described by serenity, stylish allure, and harmony—that occupants every person.

4

Chapter 4: Thrilling Outdoor Activities

Mountaineering and Rock Getting Over Endeavors

Mountaineering and shaking getting over represent the thrill and trouble of open-air investigation, furnishing people with the opportunity to go up against and evaluate their physical and mental limits despite the absolute most imposing and rough landscapes in the world. Adrenaline-actuating attempts, for example, scaling snow-covered tops and transcending rock mountains, expect climbers to have strength, aptitude, and boldness to cross vertical surfaces and defeat apparently unrealistic obstructions.

The allure of mountaineering and rock climbing lives in the identity assurance and accomplishment that come about because of climbing to exceptional levels and conquering impressive obstructions. Each rising, whether it be navigating uncovered ridgelines, arranging bone-chilling precipices, or scaling sheer stone countenances, is a test that expects climbers to show their ability, resolve, and cooperative capacities. By diving profoundly, they uncover inert strength and versatility that they previously had no clue existed.

Notwithstanding, mountaineering and rock getting over are about something other than arriving at the highest point; they are likewise about fostering a significant relationship with nature. Climbers are significantly lowered by the may and wonderfulness of the mountains as they rise to the raised environment of high-height tops and become engaged in the untamed magnificence of snow-capped scenes. They create a fresh found reverence for the sensitive balance of life that wins in these separated and threatening environmental elements.

Besides, rock getting over and mountaineering outings furnish bold people with a chance to rise above the impediments forced by society and rediscover the freedom and feeling of the regular world. Climbers look for comfort in the wild's peacefulness and isolation, whether they are on a high mountaintop, delighting in the greatness of the daybreak, or noticing far-reaching vistas from a cliffside roost. In doing so, they experience a significant reconnection with themselves and their regular habitat.

Notwithstanding, what could be viewed as the most significant advantage of rock climbing and mountaineering attempts is the friendship and associations framed among individual climbers as they, as a whole, get through the victories and difficulties experienced all through the campaign. Participating in exercises, for example, petitioning while belaying a sidekick on a difficult pitch, describing stories around an open-air fire, or recognizing a victorious culmination on the whole fashion means persevering through unions and memories that rise above the finish of the endeavor.

Essentially, mountaineering and rock-getting-over undertakings act as a demonstration of the dauntless idea of the human soul and the immortal allure of the normal world. Participating in risings of impressive levels or navigating steep precipices, each climb involves a journey of contemplation and transformation, convincing climbers to outperform their past limits and disclose their total capacities as they explore the upward domain with enthusiasm, resolve, stunningness, and wonder.

Endeavors of Whitewater Boating and Kayaking

Whitewater boating and kayaking journeys furnish daredevils with the chance to cross the tempestuous flows of the absolute most stunning streams on earth, drenching themselves in the untamed quality and imposing power of these streams. Participating in elating exercises like agitating whitewater and exploring hazardous rapids expects paddlers to have excellent ability, nimbleness, and practical dexterity to overcome considerable difficulties and succeed.

The allure of whitewater boating and kayaking lives in the strengthening flood of adrenaline that goes with the test of crossing the uncontrolled and fierce flows of a furious waterway. Each second spent on the waterway is an invigorating excursion, loaded with expectation, marvel, and spectacular potential because of the imposing powers of nature. This is exemplified by, for example, frothing whitewater, rock-flung rapids, and restricted chutes and drops.

Notwithstanding, the essence of whitewater boating and kayaking rises above simple rapids authority; it involves laying out significant and critical compatibility with the climate. While crossing pristine wild, paddlers become fascinated by the waterway's visual, hear-able, and material encounters, fostering an improved esteem for the unpredictable reliance of organic entities that possess its fringe and are lowered in its waters.

Besides, kayaking and whitewater boating journeys furnish fearless people with a chance to rise above the difficulties and monotonies of contemporary society and drench themselves in the freedom and fervor of nature. By reconnecting with themselves and the normal world in a significant way, paddlers find comfort in the effortlessness and serenity of life on the waterway, whether they are rowing through distant gulches, setting up camp under the stars, or sharing stories around a huge fire.

In any case, the fellowship and bonds framed among paddlers during whitewater boating and kayaking undertakings might be their most noteworthy prize, as they experience similar victories and troubles all through the journey. Participating in exercises like synchronized rowing through fierce rapids, helping an individual paddler save an upset boat, or recognizing a fruitful drop on a difficult stretch of waterway, all in all, means persevering through recollections and partnerships that continue quite a ways past the finish of the campaign.

In a general sense, kayaking and whitewater boating trips act as a demonstration of the getting-through charm of nature and the flexibility of the human soul. When faced with violent rapids or serene flows, each oar stroke connotes an endeavor of self-investigation and transformation, convincing paddlers to outperform their apparent limits and sincerely value the waterway's untainted magnificence with intensity, resolve, and wonder.

Experiencing Surfing Legendary Waves in Remote Locations

Surfing renowned waves in remote locations encapsulates the exhilaration and appeal of outdoor exploration, providing riders with the opportunity to ride among the most renowned and formidable waves globally. Across unspoiled tropical coastlines and remote, rugged shorelines, these exhilarating activities immerse surfers in the unadulterated might and splendor of the ocean, offering a thrilling respite from the monotony of daily life.

The appeal of riding legendary waves resides in the sensation of liberation and excitement one experiences when harnessing the ocean's energy and riding its formidable surges. Surfers have the opportunity to establish a connection with the elemental forces of nature and fleetingly experience unadulterated bliss with each wave, whether they are executing graceful turns on glassy walls or charging down towering barrels.

Be that as it may, the quest for adrenaline isn't the main justification for riding Amazing; one must likewise submerge oneself in the worldwide woven artwork of surf culture and history. Different objections brag particular ambiances and flavors, impacted by the surfers who have navigated their coasts, including the eminent rushes of Hawaii's North Shore, the confined reefs of Indonesia, and the rough shores of South Africa.

Furthermore, in pursuit of the ideal wave, sailing legendary waves provides surfers with an opportunity to venture into uncharted territories and exceed their personal limits. Surfers, whether venturing out on solitary excursions to remote island paradises or participating in group expeditions to uncharted breaks, are engrossed in the exhilaration of discovery. Driven by an unquenchable thirst for adventure, they pursue swells and search out hidden spots.

However, what could be considered the most valuable benefit of surfing legendary swells is the sense of community and camaraderie that develops among surfers as they experience the same highs and lows as the surfer lifestyle. Engaging in activities such as wave trading, storytelling around a beach bonfire, or simply lounging and surfing together fosters enduring connections that transcend the transient nature of the waves.

Surfing renowned waves in remote locations can be likened to an expedition of inquiry and revelation, where each surfed wave serves as evidence of the enduring strength of the human condition and the enduring allure of the sea. Each riding meeting, whether it be pursuing the substance of an epic wave or cutting turns on a confined reef break, presents a chance to rise above our own restrictions and experience the pure enjoyment of wave riding in a portion of the world's most unblemished and separated areas.

Skydiving and Paragliding in Amazing Scenes

Paragliding and skydiving, when performed in the midst of stunning views, embody the delight and thrill of outside investigation by furnishing members with an unrivaled chance to climb through the climate and gain a remarkable viewpoint on the world. Taking part in elating exercises, for example, dropping through tremendous blue skies or rising magnificent mountain ranges, addresses a combination of human experience and gives an unrivaled feeling of autonomy and opportunity.

The appeal of skydiving and paragliding resides in the exhilaration and sensation of weightlessness that result from challenging the force of gravity and embracing the natural world. Perilously navigating through the atmosphere propelled by gentle thermal currents or hurtling towards the planet at maximum speed, every flight provides individuals with an opportunity to partake in the unadulterated delight of flight and access an innate sense of wonderment that predates the dawn of humanity.

However, the primary objective of paragliding and skydiving is not merely to experience the exhilaration of the jump; it is also to behold the splendor and magnificence of the natural world from a vantage point that is rarely granted to individuals. Each flight gives members a one-of-a kind and significant chance to lay out an association with the earth, acquiring a more profound appreciation for its magnificence and variety. The skylines lengthen from the far-reaching vistas of rough mountain peaks to the intricate interwoven pattern of fields and backwoods that lie beneath.

What's more, paragliding and skydiving give people the amazing chance to challenge themselves in novel and exciting ways, permitting them to wander past their usual ranges of familiarity. Whether sliding from a plane at 10,000 feet or wandering into a strange area from a mountainside, members are stood up to with their most significant feelings of trepidation and frailties. By conquering these obstructions, they can achieve a significant feeling of strengthening and freedom that is genuinely life-changing.

Notwithstanding, what might be viewed as the most important advantage of paragliding and skydiving is the feeling of brotherhood and shared experience that it creates among the people who participate in these elating exercises. These common encounters, for example, trading high-fives and adrenaline-filled stories following an effective jump or holding over the thrill of taking off through the skies, manufacture perseverance through associations that endure well past the exhaustion of the adrenaline.

Essentially, skydiving and paragliding in amazing scenes act as proof of the getting-through charm of the sky and the unflinching assurance of the human soul. Each flight, whether climbing snow-covered tops or plummeting through the mists, presents a potential chance to lay out a significant association with a higher power and experience the pure joy of a trip over probably the most stunning and sensational territories in the world.

Safaris of Untamed Life and Vivid Nature Encounters

Through untamed life safaris and vivid nature encounters, fearless people can submerge themselves in the wonders, sounds, and sights of the wild, laying out an association with the regular world in its most flawless and untamed state. Taking part in bold undertakings, for example, following slippery hunters in the African savannah or noticing uncommon species in far-off rainforests, offers an unrivaled chance to acquire knowledge about the wonderful variety and quality of the world's most biodiverse environments.

The allure of untamed life trips and vivid nature encounters dwells in the chance to notice natural life right at home, unhampered by human obstruction or bondage. Each experience gives a chance to observe slippery large felines slinking through thick wilderness undergrowth, witness crowds of elephants openly meandering the savannah, or witness cases of dolphins playing in perfect waters. Such encounters summon a significant feeling of wonderment and love for the normal world and its occupants.

Be that as it may, untamed life trips and vivid nature encounters include more than simply elevated perception; they additionally require dynamic commitment to endeavors to defend imperiled species and monitor delicate biological systems. Through their support of capable ecotourism drives and untamed life protection attempts, travelers can contribute to the safeguarding and security of the territories and species that are basic to these encounters. This can ensure that impending generations will see the wonders of nature.

Moreover, untamed life trips and vivid nature encounters furnish valiant people with a chance to restore a significant association with themselves and the world while separating from the tensions and redirections of contemporary presence. Members gain a recharged appreciation for the relationship of all living things as they become engaged in the sights, sounds, and scents of the regular world while investigating far-off wild regions by walking, by boat, or in a safari vehicle.

Be that as it may, the most significant advantage of untamed life safaris and vivid nature encounters might be the significant feeling of surprise and stunningness one gets after viewing the wonder and assortment of presence in their most perfect state. Whether valuing the multifaceted wing examples of a butterfly, hearing the hypnotizing call of a far-off wolf, or seeing the greatness of a breaking humpback whale, each experience confers a permanent comprehension to members in regards to the significant and tricky nature of life on our planet.

Untamed life safaris and complete nature encounters act as a significant demonstration of the faithful soul of investigation and the immortal charm of the regular habitat. Investigating far-off wild districts in quest for buried treasures, following untamed life through thick wilderness, or navigating tremendous savannahs in quest for tricky hunters—each try gives a chance to lay out an association with a substance past ourselves and observe the brilliance and stunningness of the normal world.

5

Chapter 5: Immersing in Cultural Experiences

Partaking in Customary Services and Ceremonies

Partaking in customary services and ceremonies is an entryway to drenching oneself in the rich embroidery of culture and legacy that characterizes an objective. Whether it's seeing a holy dance performed by native clans, partaking in a customary tea service in Japan, or participating in a strict celebration in India, these vivid encounters offer explorers an opportunity to interface with the otherworldly and social practices that have molded networks for ages.

The charm of taking part in conventional services and ceremonies lies in the chance to acquire knowledge of the convictions, values, and customs that characterize a culture. As explorers witness the perplexing ceremonies and respected rehearsals that went down through hundreds of years, they gain a more profound comprehension and appreciation for the significant feeling of otherworldliness and interconnectedness that pervades numerous conventional social orders.

Besides, taking part in conventional functions and ceremonies offers voyagers an opportunity to form significant associations with neighborhood networks and gain firsthand information on their lifestyle. Whether it's helping out in getting ready contributions for a strict function or participating in a dance circle with individuals from a native clan, these common encounters make obligations of fellowship and brotherhood that rise above language and social hindrances.

In any case, maybe the best prize for partaking in customary services and ceremonies lies in the feeling of miracle and wonder that comes from seeing the magnificence and force of human articulation in its most perfect structure. Whether it's the mesmerizing cadence of drums at an ancestral get-together, the frightful tunes of a holy serenade, or the many-sided developments of a customary dance, these snapshots of social submersion contact the spirit and have an enduring effect on the hearts and brains of explorers.

Fundamentally, partaking in customary services and ceremonies is an excursion of disclosure and association, where each custom performed and each custom noticed offers a window into the spirit of a culture. Whether it's respecting the progenitors, praising the changing of the seasons, or denoting life's achievements, these immortal customs help us to remember the common humanity that ties us generally together and the widespread longing to track down importance and reason in our general surroundings.

Gaining high-quality specialties from neighborhood bosses

Gaining high-quality specialties from nearby experts gives an exceptional chance to dig into the social legacy and imaginative customs of an objective, submerging oneself in the craftsmanship and inventiveness that have been passed down through the ages. Whether it's earthenware making in a distant town, winding around perplexing materials on a customary loom, or cutting many-sided plans into wood or stone, these active encounters offer explorers an opportunity to associate with the imaginative soul of a local area and gain understanding into the abilities and procedures that characterize its social personality.

The charm of learning about high-quality specialties lies in the potential to acquire a more profound appreciation for the craftsmanship and masterfulness that go into making handcrafted products. As voyagers work close by neighborhood craftsmen, they gain firsthand information on the revered methods and careful scrupulousness that are normal for customary craftsmanship, acquiring a newly discovered appreciation for the expertise and devotion expected to dominate these old expressions.

Besides, gaining high-quality specialties from neighborhood aces offers explorers an opportunity to draw on the social legacy and character of an objective in a significant and legitimate manner. Whether it's finding out about the imagery and importance behind customary themes or understanding the role of specialties in the everyday existence and ceremonies of a local area, these vivid encounters give bits of knowledge into the rich embroidery of history, culture, and custom that characterizes a spot.

Yet, maybe the best compensation for learning high-quality specialties lies in the feeling of fulfillment and achievement that comes from making something with one's own hands. Whether it's molding dirt into a vessel, meshing string into texture, or cutting wood into many-sided plans, the demonstration of creation cultivates a feeling of association with the material world and a more profound appreciation for the magnificence and intricacy of the normal world.

Generally, gaining high-quality specialties from neighborhood aces is an excursion of imagination and disclosure, where each brushstroke, each join, and each etch mark offer a brief look into the spirit of a culture. Whether it's learning a customary art as a method for safeguarding social legacy or basically for the purpose of self-articulation and self-improvement, these involved encounters offer voyagers an opportunity to interface with an option that could be more significant than themselves and leave an enduring tradition of social trade and understanding.

Cooking and Eating with the Native Peoples Group

Cooking and eating with native networks offers voyagers a remarkable chance to investigate the culinary practices and social legacy of an objective in a profoundly vivid manner. From get-together fixings in the neighborhood market to planning customary dishes close by nearby cooks, these culinary encounters give knowledge into the flavors, strategies, and customs that have supported networks for ages.

WANDERLUST UNLEASHED

The charm of cooking and eating with native networks lies in the potential to connect every one of the faculties and experience the genuine quintessence of a culture through its food. Whether it's relishing the perplexing kinds of hot curry in India, examining the fragile surfaces of high-quality tortillas in Mexico, or enjoying the natural lavishness of a conventional stew in Africa, each dish recounts a story and offers a sample of the social embroidery that makes an objective extraordinary.

Besides, cooking and feasting with native networks offer explorers an opportunity to form significant associations with nearby individuals and gain insight into their lifestyle. Whether it's sharing stories and chuckling over a common feast or finding out about the social meaning of specific fixings and dishes, these common encounters create obligations of kinship and fellowship that rise above language and social hindrances.

Yet, maybe the best compensation for cooking and eating with native networks lies in the feeling of the local area and having a place that comes from fellowshipping together and partaking in the customs of food and friendliness. Whether it's partaking in a conventional cooking class, joining a family for a home-prepared dinner, or going to a gala or celebration, these common encounters make recollections that persist through lengthy after the plates have been cleared and the dishes washed.

Fundamentally, cooking and feasting with native networks is an excursion of investigation and association, where each dinner shared and each recipe learned offers a window into the substance of a culture. Whether it's learning the craft of making customary dishes for the purpose of social trade or basically partaking in the straightforward delight of good food and great organization, these culinary encounters offer voyagers an opportunity to interface with an option that could be more significant than themselves and gain a more profound appreciation for the rich variety of the world's societies.

Investigating Authentic Locales and Old Remnants

Investigating verifiable destinations and old remains is similar to venturing back in time, offering voyagers an opportunity to follow the strides of past developments and uncover the secrets of former periods. From superb pyramids and stupendous castles to disintegrating sanctuaries and failing to remember urban communities, these archeological marvels are windows into the rich embroidery of mankind's set of experiences, giving a substantial association with individuals and societies that preceded us.

The charm of investigating verifiable destinations and antiquated ruins lies in the feeling of marvel and wonder that comes from seeing the great accomplishments of past human advancements. Whether wondering about the accuracy of the design of an old water system, unraveling the perplexing carvings of a sanctuary wall, or envisioning the clamoring life of a long-deserted city, each site offers a brief look into the inventiveness, innovativeness, and versatility of the human soul.

Besides, investigating verifiable destinations and old vestiges offers explorers an opportunity to acquire an understanding of the social, political, and strict designs that formed the world as far as we might be concerned today. Whether it's finding out about the ascent and fall of domains, concentrating on the workmanship and engineering of a former period, or interpreting the images and engravings abandoned by old societies, these vivid encounters give a more profound comprehension of the powers that have molded human development over centuries.

However, maybe the best compensation for investigating verifiable locales and old vestiges lies in the feeling of association and congruity that comes from strolling in the strides of the people who preceded us. Whether it's feeling overwhelmed before the disintegrating city survives from a once-extraordinary city or following the layout of an old landmark with one's fingertips, these experiences with the past help us to remember our common humanity and the perseverance through tradition of the civic establishments that have gone previously.

Basically, investigating verifiable locales and old remnants is an excursion of disclosure and reflection, where each stone, each engraving, and each curio recounts a story. Whether it's unwinding the secrets of lost civilizations or basically wondering about the progression of time, these archeological marvels offer voyagers an opportunity to interface with an option that could be more significant than themselves and gain a more profound appreciation for the rich embroidery of mankind's set of experiences that ties us generally together.

Going to Celebrations and Far-Reaching Developments

Going to celebrations and widespread developments is an energetic and dynamic method for drenching oneself in the heartbeat of an objective, offering voyagers an opportunity to commend the practices, customs, and ceremonies that characterize a local area's personality. From bright road marches and energetic live concerts to grave strict functions and customary dance exhibitions, these social get-togethers give a window into the spirit of a culture, welcoming members to participate in the celebrations and offer in the delight and brotherhood of the event.

The charm of going to celebrations and comprehensive developments lies in the chance to encounter the dynamic quality and variety of human articulation in its many structures. Whether it's seeing the complex ensembles and elaborate floats of a fair procession, inspecting the fascinating kinds of road food sellers at a night market, or moving under the stars to the rhythms of unrecorded music, every occasion offers a blowout for the faculties and an opportunity to interface with the social legacy of an objective.

Besides, going to celebrations and comprehensive developments offers explorers an opportunity to form significant associations with nearby networks and gain knowledge about their lifestyle. Whether it's participating in a customary dance circle, taking part in a strict parade, or electing to assist with sorting out a local area occasion, these common encounters create obligations of fellowship and kinship that rise above language and social obstructions.

In any case, maybe the best compensation for going to celebrations and comprehensive developments lies in the feeling of festivity and shared humanity that comes from meeting up to praise the things that join us as animal varieties. Whether it's recognizing a reap celebration, regarding the changing of the seasons, or celebrating strict occasions and achievements, these get-togethers help us to remember the widespread craving to track down bliss, significance, and association in our general surroundings.

Fundamentally, going to celebrations and comprehensive developments is an excursion of festivity and revelation, where each dance, each melody, and each ceremonial offer a brief look into the essence of a culture. Whether it's participating in the party as a method for encountering social trade or just for the purpose of partaking in the straightforward delight of good organization and happiness, these merry get-togethers offer voyagers an opportunity to interface with an option that could be more significant than themselves and gain a more profound appreciation for the rich variety of the world's societies.

6

Chapter 6: Documenting Adventures

Keeping a Movement Diary to Catch Recollections and Reflections

Keeping a movement diary is something other than reporting the spots you visit; it's a profoundly private excursion of self-disclosure and reflection that permits you to catch the essence of your undertakings and safeguard the recollections long into the future. Whether you're investigating distant places or setting out on an excursion nearer home, a movement diary fills in as a gold mine of encounters, feelings, and bits of knowledge that offer a window into the spirit of your movements.

The charm of keeping a movement diary lies in the valuable chance to catch the temporary minutes and permanent impressions that characterize your excursion. From the stunning magnificence of a dawn over the mountains to the fortunate experiences with local people in a clamoring market, every section in your diary turns into a preview of a second in time—aa memory to be esteemed and returned to at whatever point you long to remember the enchantment of your undertakings.

In any case, keeping a movement diary isn't just about recording the spots you visit; it's likewise about pondering the more profound significance and meaning of your encounters. Whether you're wrestling with the difficulties of exploring an unfamiliar culture or delighting in the delights of recently discovered companionships, your diary turns into a space for contemplation and self-articulation—aa material whereupon to investigate your considerations, sentiments, and perceptions about your general surroundings.

Besides, keeping a movement diary offers an opportunity to level up your composing abilities and develop a more profound appreciation for the craft of narrating. Whether you're making striking portrayals of the scenes you experience, writing genuine reflections on individuals you meet, or winding around together tales and stories to make a story embroidery of your excursion, your diary turns into a material for innovativeness and self-articulation—aa demonstration of the force of words to bring out feelings and move the creative mind.

In any case, maybe the best compensation for keeping a movement diary lies in the feeling of association and coherence that comes from recording your experiences continuously. Whether you're imparting your diary to loved ones back home or returning to it years later to think back about past undertakings, your diary turns into a scaffold between the past, present, and future—an unmistakable sign of the groundbreaking influence of movement to enhance our lives and expand our viewpoints in manners we never imagined.

Generally, keeping a movement diary is an excursion of self-revelation and reflection, where each word composed and each memory caught turns into a demonstration of the wealth and magnificence of the human experience. Whether you're leaving on a fabulous experience or just investigating the world on your own terrace, your diary turns into a loyal friend and comrade—aa vault of dreams, desires, and recollections that will remain with you long after the excursion has finished.

Photography Methods for Catching Shocking Scenes and Real Minutes

Photography is an amazing asset for saving the substance of your experiences, permitting you to catch the stunning excellence of scenes and the open minutes that characterize your excursion. Whether you're investigating rough mountain ranges, flawless seashores, or clamoring city roads, excelling at photography empowers you to deify the sights, sounds, and feelings of your movements exhaustively.

The charm of photography lies in its capacity to freeze a transitory second in time, permitting you to return to the sights and vibes of your movements long after you've gotten back. From the delicate tints of a nightfall painting the sky in a range of pastel tones to the rough forms of a mountain range outlined against the skyline, each photo turns into a window into the spirit of your location—aa visual sign of the excellence and miracle that anticipates the people who set out to investigate.

Yet, catching dazzling scenes and genuine minutes requires something other than picking up and firing away; it requires a comprehension of the piece, lighting, and narrating. Whether you're outlining a glorious vista with the standard of thirds, trusting that the ideal second will catch a brief demeanor on a more odd's face, or trying different things with various camera settings to accomplish the ideal impact, dominating the specialized parts of photography permits you to release your imagination and raise your pictures from simple depictions to show-stoppers.

Besides, photography offers a one-of-a kind chance to draw in with your general surroundings in a more profound and significant manner. Whether you're drenching yourself in the normal excellence of a far-off wild or recording the energetic energy of a clamoring road market, the demonstration of capturing your environmental factors urges you to dial back, notice the subtleties, and value the little snapshots of magnificence and miracle that frequently slip through the cracks in the surge of regular day-to-day existence.

In any case, maybe the best compensation of photography lies in the recollections it assists with safeguarding and the tales it assists with telling. Whether you're flipping through a photograph collection years after the fact or imparting your pictures to loved ones back home, each photo turns into an esteemed keepsake—aa substantial sign of the experiences you've had, the individuals you've met, and the spots you've investigated enroute.

Generally, photography is an excursion of investigation and disclosure, where each snap of the shade carries you one bit closer to catching the embodiment of your movements. Whether you're an old pro or a beginner devotee, the force of photography lies in its capacity to change the conventional into the unprecedented, permitting you to see the world with a new perspective, offer magnificence, and marvel with others in manners words alone can't convey.

Making Travel Recordings to Impart Encounters to Other People

Making travel recordings is a dynamic and enrapturing method for imparting your undertakings to other people, offering a visual story that rejuvenates your encounters in distinctive detail. Whether you're investigating old vestiges, traveling across thick wildernesses, or just absorbing the sights and hints of a clamoring city, travel recordings give a window into the world that permits watchers to encounter the rush and miracle of your excursion vicariously.

The charm of making travel recordings lies in their capacity to capture the substance of an objective that words and photos alone can't convey. From the general vistas of rough mountain reaches to the personal minutes imparted to local people in a clamoring market, each casing of your video recounts a story and welcomes viewers to leave on a virtual excursion of investigation and disclosure.

However, making travel recordings isn't just about displaying the magnificence of the spots you visit; it's additionally about sharing the human stories and social experiences that make every objective one of a kind. Whether you're meeting neighborhood craftsmen about their art, testing extraordinary road food with merchants, or taking part in customary services and ceremonies, your recordings become a stage for multifaceted trade and exchange—aa festival of the rich embroidery of variety that characterizes our reality.

Besides, making travel recordings offers an opportunity to level up your filmmaking abilities and release your imagination in previously unheard-of ways. Whether you're trying different things with various camera points and altering procedures or forming the ideal soundtrack to go with your recording, the most common way of creating a movement video turns into an excursion of self-articulation and imaginative investigation—aa demonstration of the force of narrating to rouse, teach, and engage.

However, maybe the best compensation for making travel recordings lies in the capacity to motivate others to leave on their own undertakings and investigate the world with open hearts and inquisitive personalities. Whether you're imparting your recordings to loved ones or transferring them to virtual entertainment stages and video-sharing sites, your recordings become a wellspring of motivation and strengthening—an update that the world is loaded with ponders ready to be found and that the best experience of everything is the excursion of self-disclosure that looks for all of us.

Fundamentally, making travel recordings is an excursion of investigation and narrating, where each casing caught and each scene shot turns into a demonstration of the excellence and variety of our planet. Whether you're recording your movements for individual happiness or imparting them to the world at large, your recordings become a heritage —an enduring demonstration of the groundbreaking force of movement to expand our perspectives, develop how we might interpret the world, and fashion associations that rise above lines and limits.

Using online entertainment and publishing content on a blog, Stages to Record Experiences

Using virtual entertainment and writing for a blog stage is a cutting-edge and open method for recording your undertakings, offering a worldwide audience an ongoing look into your movements and encounters. Whether you're sharing depictions of beautiful scenes on Instagram, writing smart reflections on your blog, or posting updates and experiences on stages like Facebook and Twitter, web-based entertainment and publishing content to a blog give a computerized journal that permits you to narrative your excursion and associate with others in manners that were unbelievable only years and years prior.

The charm of using web-based entertainment and writing for a blog stage lies in the capacity to impart your experiences to a different and sweeping crowd, immediately associating with companions, family, and individual voyagers all over the planet. Whether you're looking for movement tips and suggestions from similar fans or just imparting the features of your excursion to friends and family back home, virtual entertainment and publishing content to a blog give a stage to narrating and local area construction that rises above geological limits and social partitions.

Be that as it may, using virtual entertainment and contributing to a blog stage isn't just about communicating your encounters to the world; it's likewise about encouraging significant associations and exchange with other people who share your energy for movement and investigation. Whether you're drawing in with devotees in the remarks segment of your blog, partaking in web-based gatherings and networks committed to travel, or teaming up with individual substance makers on cooperative undertakings, virtual entertainment and publishing content to a blog offer vast open doors for association and coordinated effort that enhance your excursion and extend how you might interpret the world.

Additionally, using online entertainment and contributing to a blog stage offers an opportunity to organize and safeguard your movement recollections in a computerized design that can be returned to and shared long into the future. Whether you're looking at old presents and photographs to think back about past undertakings or gathering your number one minute into a computerized scrapbook or travelogue, web-based entertainment and publishing content to a blog give a computerized chronicle that guarantees your recollections will persevere through lengthy after your process has finished.

However, maybe the best award of using virtual entertainment and writing for a blog stage lies in the capacity to move and engage others to leave on their own experiences and investigate the world with open hearts and inquisitive personalities. Whether you're sharing travel tips and suggestions, recording your encounters with trustworthiness and validity, or essentially spreading happiness and energy through your posts and updates, virtual entertainment and publishing content to a blog become a stage for association, motivation, and strengthening that rises above lines and limits, joining explorers from varying backgrounds in a common festival of the excellence and marvel of our reality.

Basically, using virtual entertainment and contributing to a blog stage is an excursion of association and local area, where each post, remark, and collaboration turns into a demonstration of the groundbreaking force of movement to join us as a worldwide family. Whether you're imparting your undertakings to the world or essentially interfacing with other people who share your enthusiasm for investigation and revelation, web-based entertainment and publishing content to a blog become a computerized journal of your excursion—aa heritage that will persevere through lengthy after your movements have reached a conclusion.

Safeguarding Keepsakes and Trinkets to Celebrate Unique Minutes

Safeguarding keepsakes and gifts is a valued custom that permits voyagers to catch the embodiment of their undertakings and make unmistakable tokens of the exceptional minutes and encounters they've experienced enroute. Whether it's a shell gathered from a perfect oceanside, a high-quality knickknack bought from a neighborhood craftsman, or a ticket stub from a critical widespread development, these actual tokens act as unmistakable tokens of the spots you've been, the individuals you've met, and the recollections you've made.

The charm of protecting tokens and trinkets lies in their capacity to epitomize the embodiment of an objective in an actual article, changing regular things into esteemed mementos pervaded with individual importance. Whether it's a piece of adornment enhanced with a gemstone local to the district, a piece of fine art that catches the magnificence of the scene, or a garment embellished with conventional themes and plans, every trinket turns into a substantial association with the way of life, history, and customs of the spot it addresses.

Be that as it may, protecting tokens and gifts isn't just about obtaining material belongings; it's likewise about developing a more profound appreciation for our general surroundings and the individuals who inhabit them. Whether you're supporting neighborhood craftsmen and skilled workers by buying high-quality merchandise, trading presents with recently discovered companions as a token of fellowship and generosity, or basically gathering tokens and knickknacks as a method for recognizing your excursion, the demonstration of protecting keepsakes and gifts turns into a festival of the extravagance and variety of our reality.

Additionally, safeguarding keepsakes and gifts offers an opportunity to make an unmistakable record of your movements that can be returned to and valued for quite a long time into the future. Whether you're showing your gifts in a shadow box or memory container, making a scrapbook or photograph collection loaded up with keepsakes and recollections, or essentially concealing remembrances in an extraordinary box or cabinet, saving keepsakes and trinkets turns into a method for deifying your undertakings and making an enduring heritage that can be passed down from one age to another.

In any case, maybe the best award for protecting keepsakes and gifts lies in their capacity to bring out recollections and feelings long after the excursion has finished. Whether you're thinking back about the sights, sounds, and scents of a far-off land as you grasp an esteemed token or imparting stories and recollections to friends and family as you accumulate around a presentation of gifts and remembrances, the demonstration of safeguarding keepsakes and trinkets turns into a passage to remembering the wizardry and miracle of your movements over and over.

Generally, safeguarding keepsakes and gifts is an excursion of memory and importance, where each knickknack, token, and fortune turns into a demonstration of the wealth and magnificence of the human experience. Whether you're gathering trinkets as a method for honoring extraordinary minutes or basically for interfacing with the spots and individuals you experience enroute, the demonstration of protecting tokens and gifts turns into a festival of the delight, marvel, and experience that characterize the substance of movement.

Chapter 7: Overcoming Challenges and Adversity

Creating Flexibility Notwithstanding Startling Mishaps

Creating flexibility notwithstanding startling mishaps is a sign of the gutsy soul, offering explorers the strength and mettle to endure life's hardships and arise more grounded and stronger on the other side. Whether it's a failed-to-catch plane, a lost identification, or an abrupt change in plans, surprising difficulties are an unavoidable piece of the movement experience, giving explorers unexpected difficulties and hindrances that test their purpose and assurance.

The charm of creating versatility lies in the capacity to embrace difficulty as a chance for development and self-disclosure, as opposed to as a road obstruction to be dreaded or stayed away from. Rather than permitting misfortunes to crash their excursion or hose their spirits, versatile explorers view them as important growth opportunities that offer insights into their own assets and shortcomings and show significant illustrations of flexibility, determination, and the influence of strength.

In any case, creating strength isn't just about quickly returning from misfortunes; it's likewise about developing an outlook of energy and idealism that permits explorers to confront difficulties with fortitude and assurance. Whether it's rethinking negative encounters as any open doors for development, keeping a funny bone notwithstanding difficulty, or zeroing in on arrangements as opposed to harping on issues, versatile voyagers approach hindrances with a feeling of strength and cleverness that empowers them to defeat even the most overwhelming difficulties.

Besides, creating versatility offers an opportunity to produce further associations with others and fortify obligations of companionship and kinship despite misfortune. Whether looking for help from individual voyagers who have confronted comparative difficulties, tracking down comfort and support in the graciousness of outsiders, or just sharing stories and giggling over some tea, versatile explorers draw strength from their associations with others and find solace in the information that they are in good company in their battles.

However, maybe the best prize for creating strength lies in the feeling of strengthening and fearlessness that comes from conquering difficulties and affliction. Whether it's effectively exploring an unfamiliar city utilizing only a guide and a feeling of experience, tracking down savvy fixes to unforeseen issues, or essentially gathering the mental fortitude to step outside one's usual range of familiarity and embrace the obscure, strong voyagers rise out of their encounters with a recently discovered feeling of solidarity, flexibility, and certainty that stays with them long after the excursion has finished.

Generally, creating strength is an excursion of self-revelation and strengthening, where each misfortune and obstruction turns into a chance for development and change. Whether you're confronting difficulties out and about or exploring the high points and low points of day-to-day existence, the capacity to develop versatility and embrace difficulty with fortitude and assurance is a strong update that regardless of what life tosses your way, you have the strength and flexibility to conquer it and arise more grounded and stronger on the other side.

Developing Flexibility to Explore New Circumstances

Developing versatility is crucial expertise for explorers to explore new circumstances and conquer the bunch of difficulties that unavoidably emerge out and about. Whether it's exploring language boundaries in a far-off country, adapting to surprising changes in itinerary items, or adjusting to social standards and customs that vary from one's own, the capacity to stay adaptable and liberal is fundamental for flourishing in new and different conditions.

The charm of developing flexibility lies in the valuable chance to embrace vulnerability and change as impetuses for development and change. As opposed to surveying surprising difficulties as detours or mishaps, versatile voyagers consider them to be valuable chances to extend their cutoff points, expand their viewpoints, and grow their usual ranges of familiarity in manners they never imagined.

In any case, developing flexibility isn't just about responding to surprising difficulties; it's likewise about proactively searching out new encounters and pushing past one's usual range of familiarity in the quest for individual and expert development. Whether it's discovering new food varieties, submerging oneself in new traditions, or venturing beyond one's social or etymological safe place, versatile explorers embrace the obscure with a feeling of interest and experience that permits them to flourish in even the most difficult of conditions.

Besides, developing flexibility offers an opportunity to associate with neighborhood networks and individual voyagers in significant and true ways. Whether it's gaining from the flexibility and creativity of local people who have endured their own portion of difficulties or drawing strength and motivation from the brotherhood and backing of individual explorers who are exploring comparative encounters, versatility turns into a pathway to producing further associations and building enduring kinships that rise above geological and social limits.

In any case, maybe the best prize for developing versatility lies in the feeling of strengthening and fearlessness that comes from realizing that regardless of what difficulties might emerge, you have the right stuff and flexibility to defeat them. Whether it's exploring the intricacies of an unfamiliar transportation framework, settling unforeseen calculated difficulties, or basically adjusting to the back and forth movement of life out and about, versatile voyagers track down strength and development in difficulty, rising up out of each challenge more grounded, smarter, and stronger than previously.

Basically, developing versatility is an excursion of self-disclosure and strengthening, where each surprising test turns into a chance for development and change. Whether you're exploring the exciting bends in the road of another experience or essentially embracing the vulnerabilities of existence with an open heart and brain, versatility turns into a core value that permits you to flourish notwithstanding misfortune and embrace the vast conceivable outcomes that look for you out and about ahead.

Looking for Help from Nearby People Groups and Individual Explorers

Notwithstanding difficulties and misfortune, looking for help from neighborhood networks and individual explorers can be a lifesaver, offering a feeling of fortitude and fellowship that explores through difficult stretches. Whether it's requesting headings from a well-disposed neighborhood, looking for suggestions from individual voyagers in an inn, or associating with similar people through web-based gatherings and virtual entertainment gatherings, connecting for help makes an organization of partners who can offer direction, support, and help when it's most required.

The appeal of looking for help from nearby networks and individual explorers lies in the feeling of association and having a place that comes from knowing you're in good company in your battles. Whether you're wrestling with social contrasts, confronting language obstructions, or basically feeling achy to go home and awkward, realizing that there are other people who comprehend what you're going through can give solace and consolation, assisting with easing sensations of confinement and forlornness.

Be that as it may, looking for help isn't just about getting help from others; it's likewise about building significant associations and cultivating a sense of locality wherever you go. Whether it's starting up a discussion with an individual explorer on a long transport ride, going to a neighborhood comprehensive development or celebration, or chipping in with a grassroots association locally, looking for help turns into a method for overcoming any issues among outsiders and fashioning obligations of companionship and fortitude that rise above geological and social limits.

Besides, looking for help from neighborhood networks and individual explorers offers an opportunity to acquire priceless bits of knowledge and viewpoints that can assist with exploring through new circumstances and beaten difficulties with no sweat and certainty. Whether it's finding out about neighborhood customs and customs from a cordial person nearby, getting down-to-earth counsel and tips from prepared voyagers who have been from your point of view, or basically finding solace in shared encounters and stories, looking for help turns into a wellspring of shrewdness and direction that can have a significant effect in exploring the ups and downs of movement.

Yet, maybe the best compensation for looking for help from neighborhood networks and individual explorers lies in the feeling of strengthening and versatility that comes from realizing you have an emotionally supportive network to rest on when difficulties go crazy. Whether it's getting some assistance from an outsider in a period of scarcity or offering help and consolation to other people who are confronting their own difficulties, looking for help turns into a corresponding trade of thoughtfulness and sympathy that reinforces bonds and encourages a feeling of fortitude that rises above lines and limits.

Fundamentally, looking for help from nearby networks and individual voyagers is an excursion of association and joint effort, where each collaboration turns into a chance to construct spans, fashion fellowships, and make an organization of partners who can help explore through the promising and less promising times of movement. Whether you're looking for reasonable help, consistent encouragement, or essentially a feeling of having a place in a world that can frequently feel overpowering and dubious, looking for help turns into an encouraging sign and an update that regardless of where you are on the planet, you're rarely really alone.

Embracing the Illustrations Gained from Defeating Difficulties

Embracing the illustrations gained from defeating difficulties is a major part of self-improvement and advancement, offering important bits of knowledge and insight that can enhance each part of our lives. Whether it's exploring through unforeseen misfortunes out and about, defying fears and vulnerabilities, or beating obstructions that test our versatility and resolve, each challenge we face turns into a chance for self-disclosure and change—an opportunity to develop strength, flexibility, and shrewdness that will work well for us in all parts of our lives.

The charm of embracing the examples gained from conquering provokes lies in the chance to uncover stowed-away qualities and abilities that we might not have realized we had. Whether it's finding a newly discovered feeling of versatility and assurance notwithstanding difficulty or taking advantage of our inventiveness and creativity to find imaginative answers for complex issues, each challenge we defeat turns into a venturing stone on the way to self-revelation and strengthening—an indication of the profundity and expansiveness of our own true capacity.

Yet, embracing the examples gained from defeating difficulties isn't just about self-awareness and improvement; it's likewise about encouraging a more profound feeling of sympathy and empathy for other people who might be confronting their own battles. Whether it's a listening ear and a shoulder to rest on for an individual voyager out of luck or sharing our own accounts of wins and flexibility to move and elevate others, each challenge we defeat turns into a wellspring of solidarity and motivation that can swell outwards to make positive change on the planet.

Besides, embracing the examples gained from defeating moves offers an opportunity to develop an outlook of appreciation for the actual excursion. Whether it's pondering the manners by which each challenge has assisted us with developing and developing as people or offering thanks for the help and support we've gotten from others enroute, each challenge we defeat turns into a sign of the excellence and versatility of the human soul—aa demonstration of the force of persistence and assurance to change misfortune into a potential open door and development.

However, maybe the best compensation for embracing the examples gained from defeating difficulties lies in the feeling of strengthening and self-assurance that comes from realizing that regardless of what snags might come our way, we have the flexibility and inward solidarity to beat them. Whether it's confronting the vulnerabilities of movement with mental fortitude and elegance or standing up to the difficulties of day-to-day existence with versatility and assurance, each challenge we defeat turns into our very own demonstration of inward strength and an update that we are fit for accomplishing significance notwithstanding difficulty.

Fundamentally, embracing the examples gained from beating difficulties is an excursion of self-revelation and strengthening, where each impediment turns into a chance for development and change. Whether we're exploring through the ups and downs of movement or defying the difficulties of day-to-day existence, each challenge we defeat turns into a demonstration of the strength of the human soul and an update that, with boldness, assurance, and tirelessness, we can conquer any hindrance that holds us up.

Tracking down strength and development in misfortune

Finding strength and development in difficulty is a demonstration of the flexibility of the human soul, offering a significant chance for individual change and strengthening. When confronted with difficulties that test our cutoff points and push us beyond our usual ranges of familiarity, we have the decision to either surrender to gloom or adapt to the situation with mental fortitude, assurance, and elegance. It is at these times of affliction that we find the profundities of our own inward strength and flexibility, taking advantage of supplies of mental fortitude and versatility that we might not have known existed.

The charm of finding strength and development in difficulty lies in the potential chance to change our battles into venturing stones for self-awareness and advancement. Whether it's defeating actual obstructions on a difficult climb, exploring through social false impressions in an unfamiliar land, or enduring through private difficulties and misfortunes, every misfortune we face turns into a potential chance to develop strength, fearlessness, and internal harmony that will work well for us in all parts of our lives.

In any case, finding strength and development in misfortune isn't just about defeating snags; it's additionally about embracing the actual excursion and tracking down importance and reason amidst life's difficulties. Whether it's finding newly discovered qualities and gifts that we never realized we had or acquiring a more profound appreciation for the endowments and valuable open doors that encompass us, every misfortune we defeat turns into an impetus for self-improvement and change—an update that even in our most obscure minutes, there is light and expect to be found.

In addition, finding strength and development in difficulty offers an opportunity to motivate and elevate other people who might be confronting their own battles. Whether it's sharing our accounts of wins and flexibility to energize others on their own excursion or offering backing and support to those out of luck, every difficulty we defeat turns into a wellspring of motivation and strengthening that can swell outwards to make positive change on the planet.

However, maybe the best compensation for finding strength and development in difficulty lies in the feeling of strengthening and self-assurance that comes from realizing that regardless of what difficulties might come our way, we have the inward strength and flexibility to beat them. Whether it's confronting the vulnerabilities of movement with fortitude and elegance or standing up to the difficulties of day-to-day existence with versatility and assurance, every difficulty we defeat turns into our very own demonstration of internal strength and an update that we are equipped for accomplishing significance despite misfortune.

Generally, finding strength and development in difficulty is an excursion of self-revelation and strengthening, where each impediment turns into a chance for development and change. Whether we're exploring through the ups and downs of movement or facing the difficulties of daily existence, every difficulty we defeat turns into a demonstration of the flexibility of the human soul and an update that, with mental fortitude, assurance, and determination, we can beat any snag that hinders us.

8

Chapter 8: Sustainable and Responsible Travel Practices

Grasping the Standards of Supportable Travel and Its Effect on Neighborhood People Groups and Biological Systems

Understanding the standards of reasonable travel is fundamental for reliable voyagers who wish to limit their effect on the climate and support the prosperity of nearby networks and biological systems. Manageable travel encompasses an all-encompassing methodology that thinks about the social, monetary, and ecological ramifications of the travel industry, expecting to safeguard normal assets, safeguard social legacy, and cultivate positive connections among voyagers and host networks.

The charm of understanding maintainable travel lies in the acknowledgment that our activities as voyagers have sweeping results that reach beyond our singular encounters. From the fossil fuel byproducts created by transportation to the waste delivered by the travel industry, the effect of movement on the climate can be huge and dependable. By understanding the standards of reasonable travel, voyagers can pursue informed decisions that limit their natural impression and advance dependable stewardship of the spots they visit.

Yet, understanding practical travel isn't just about limiting mischief; it's additionally about augmenting the positive advantages of the travel industry for nearby networks and biological systems. Maintainable travel looks to enable host networks by setting out financial open doors, safeguarding social practices, and advancing preservation endeavors that safeguard biodiversity and regular territories. By understanding the interconnectedness of the travel industry and nearby livelihoods, explorers can uphold drives that advance manageability and social value, guaranteeing that their presence adds to the prosperity of host networks as opposed to diminishing it.

Besides, understanding reasonable travel offers an opportunity to develop a more profound appreciation for the spots we visit and the individuals who call them home. By finding out about the natural and social difficulties confronting host networks, explorers can acquire an understanding of the mind-boggling elements of the travel industry and foster a feeling of compassion and regard for the different societies and environments they experience. Through significant commitment with nearby occupants and support in economic travel industry exercises, explorers can fashion associations that rise above social and topographical limits, encouraging shared understanding and regard between their networks and guests.

Yet, maybe the best prize for understanding reasonable travel lies in the feeling of satisfaction and fulfillment that comes from realizing that our movements definitely affect the world. Whether it's supporting nearby organizations and craftsmen, chipping in with protection associations, or upholding economical travel industry strategies, voyagers can assume a significant role in molding a more practical and evenhanded future for all. By understanding the standards of economical travel and integrating them into our excursions, we can become ministers of change, rousing others to emulate our example and have an effect on the planet with each outing in turn.

Fundamentally, understanding feasible travel is an excursion of mindfulness and obligation, where each decision we make as explorers has the ability to shape the world for the better or in negative ways. Whether we're investigating remote areas or wandering into our own lawn, our movements can possibly leave an enduring effect on the spots we visit and the individuals we experience. By understanding the standards of feasible travel and embracing them as core values, we can guarantee that our processes add to the prosperity of both present and future generations, abandoning a tradition of stewardship and regard for the planet and its occupants.

Carrying out Eco-Accommodating Practices to Limit Natural Impression While Voyaging

Executing eco-accommodating practices is fundamental for limiting our natural impression while voyaging and protecting the regular magnificence and biological honesty of the spots we visit. With the rising consciousness of environmental change and ecological corruption, voyagers have an obligation to embrace reasonable ways of behaving that lessen their effect on the world and advance protection endeavors in objections all over the planet.

The charm of executing eco-accommodating practices lies in the potential chance to have a beneficial outcome for the wellbeing and essentialness of our planet. From lessening energy utilization and waste creation to supporting organizations and associations that focus on natural supportability, each eco-accommodating activity we require adds to the aggregate work to secure and protect the Earth for people in the future.

However, executing eco-accommodating practices isn't just about rolling out little improvements to our everyday propensities; it's likewise about embracing a mentality of natural stewardship and obligation that directs our activities as explorers. Whether selecting eco-accommodating facilities limits energy and water utilization, picking reasonable transportation choices like strolling, cycling, or utilizing public transportation, or lessening single-use plastics and dispensable things while out and about, each choice we make can possibly have a constructive outcome on the climate.

Besides, executing eco-accommodating practices offers an opportunity to show others how it is done and move others to take on additional manageable ways of behaving in their own lives. Whether it's imparting tips and proposals to individual explorers, taking part in local area tidy-up endeavors, or supporting nearby protection drives, voyagers can use their aggregate impact to advocate for positive change and bring issues to light about the significance of ecological supportability.

In any case, maybe the best compensation for executing eco-accommodating practices lies in the feeling of satisfaction and fulfillment that comes from realizing that our activities are having an effect. Whether it's seeing the magnificence of a flawless normal scene or seeing the grins on the essences of nearby inhabitants who benefit from maintainable the travel industry drives, each eco-accommodating activity we take reaffirms our obligation to safeguarding the planet and protecting its miracles for people in the future to appreciate.

Basically, executing eco-accommodating practices is an excursion of care and deliberateness, where each decision we make as voyagers has the ability to shape the fate of our planet. By embracing a mentality of ecological stewardship and obligation, we can guarantee that our movements abandon a tradition of preservation and manageability—aa demonstration of our obligation to safeguard the Earth and its occupants, presently and for a long time into the future.

Supporting Neighborhood Economies and Networks Through Dependable The travel industry drives

Supporting neighborhood economies and networks through dependable travel industry drives is central to cultivating an economical turn of events and enabling occupants to raise objections all over the planet. As explorers, we have the potential to contribute decisively to the financial prosperity of host networks by disparaging privately claimed organizations, taking part in social trade, and supporting drives that focus on the requirements and goals of neighborhood occupants.

The charm of supporting neighborhood economies and networks lies in the acknowledgment that the travel industry can be a strong power for monetary development and neediness mitigation when overseen capably. By spending our cash at privately possessed inns, cafés, shops, and visit administrators, we can guarantee that a more noteworthy portion of the travel industry dollars stays inside the local area, making position, invigorating monetary turn of events, and working on the personal satisfaction of occupants.

Yet, supporting nearby economies and networks isn't just about monetary effects; it's additionally about encouraging significant associations and social trade among voyagers and host networks. Whether it's finding out about conventional specialties and customs from nearby craftsmen, partaking in local area drives and exercises, or chipping in with grassroots associations that address neighborhood needs, voyagers have the chance to draw in with occupants in manners that advance common figuring out, regard, and appreciation for assorted societies and viewpoints.

Besides, supporting neighborhood economies and networks offers an opportunity to address the social and natural difficulties confronting objections all over the planet. By putting resources into local area-based travel industry drives that focus on natural maintainability, social value, and social protection, voyagers can add to the drawn-out prosperity of host networks while limiting adverse consequences for the climate and neighborhood lifestyle.

In any case, maybe the best prize for supporting neighborhood economies and networks lies in the feeling of satisfaction and association that comes from realizing that our movements emphatically affect the existences of others. Whether it's seeing the grins on the essences of neighborhood occupants who benefit from the travel industry's related pay or seeing the strength and imagination of networks that have met up to address shared difficulties, each demonstration of help reaffirms our obligation to capable travel and our faith in the force of the travel industry to make positive change on the planet.

Basically, supporting nearby economies and networks is an excursion of fortitude and strengthening, where each dollar spent and each communication shared turns into an impetus for practical turns of events and social advancement. By focusing on the necessities and yearnings of nearby occupants in our movements, we can assist with making a reality where the travel industry benefits everybody—where explorers and host networks flourish as one with one another and the normal world around us.

Taking Part in Social Trade and Regarding Nearby Traditions and Customs

Participating in social trade and regarding neighborhood customs is fundamental for encouraging common understanding, regard, and appreciation among voyagers and host networks. As guests to unfamiliar terrains, we have the potential to immerse ourselves in the rich embroidered artwork of societies and customs that make every objective extraordinary, gaining from neighborhood occupants and sharing our own points of view and encounters consequently.

The charm of participating in social trade lies in the potential to expand our viewpoints and extend our perspective through significant associations with individuals from various foundations and viewpoints. Whether it's taking part in customary functions and ceremonies, testing neighborhood food, or finding out about the set of experiences and legacy of a specific spot, social trade offers a window into the substance of an objective, improving our movements with profundity and importance beyond the surface attractions.

However, captivating in social trade isn't just about encountering new things; it's additionally about extending admiration and appreciation for the traditions and customs of the networks we visit. By finding out about nearby decorum and standards, regarding hallowed locales and images, and respecting the desires of occupants, explorers can exhibit their obligation to be mindful and moral in the travel industry rehearsals that focus on social awareness and modesty.

Besides, engaging in social trade offers an opportunity to separate boundaries and construct extensions of understanding and sympathy between individuals from various societies and foundations. Whether it's offering stories and chuckling to local people over a feast, partaking in local area drives and occasions, or just starting up discussions with outsiders in the city, social trade turns into an impetus for building associations that rise above language, identity, and nationality.

In any case, maybe the best compensation for taking part in social trade lies in the feeling of association and having a place that comes from fashioning significant associations with individuals from around the world. Whether shaping companionships endure forever, acquiring bits of knowledge and points of view that challenge our suppositions and expand our perspectives, or basically feeling a feeling of connection and fortitude with individual people, social trade turns into a wellspring of happiness and satisfaction that improves our lives in ways we never imagined.

Basically, captivating in social trade is an excursion of revelation and association, where each connection turns into a valuable chance to learn, develop, and advance as people and as worldwide residents. By moving toward our movements with an open heart and a receptive outlook, we can fabricate scaffolds of understanding and compassion that rise above social limits and join us in our common humankind, making a reality where variety is praised, contrasts are regarded, and everybody has a spot at the table.

Adding to Preservation Endeavors and Safeguarding Normal and Social Legacy Locales

Adding to preservation endeavors and safeguarding regular and social legacy destinations is fundamental to protecting the magnificence and uprightness of the spots we visit for people in the future to appreciate. As voyagers, we affect the climate and promote the safeguarding of appreciated milestones, biological systems, and social fortunes that are in danger from overdevelopment, contamination, and different dangers.

The appeal of adding to protection endeavors lies in the valuable chance to be stewards of the Earth, shielding its normal miracles and social fortunes to assist all. Whether it's partaking in untamed life preservation projects, chipping in with associations that safeguard jeopardized species and living spaces, or supporting drives that advance maintainable the travel industry rehearses, explorers can assume an essential part in saving the biodiversity and biological equilibrium of our planet.

However, adding to preservation endeavors isn't just about safeguarding the climate; it's additionally about regarding the social legacy of the networks we visit. By supporting the safeguarding of memorable locales, landmarks, and consecrated milestones, explorers can assist in guaranteeing that people in the future have the valuable chance to gain from and value the rich embroidered artwork of mankind's set of experiences and culture that has molded our reality.

Besides, adding to protection endeavors offers an opportunity to teach and motivate others to make a move in the interest of the planet. Whether it's sharing data and assets about natural issues and protection drives, bringing issues to light through online entertainment and local area efforts, or showing others how it's done through our own manageable ways of behaving and rehearsing, voyagers can be strong backers for positive change on the planet.

In any case, maybe the best prize for adding to protection endeavors lies in the feeling of satisfaction and reason that comes from realizing that our activities are having an effect. Whether it's seeing the recuperation of an imperiled species, seeing the reclamation of a corrupted biological system, or encountering the delight and appreciation of nearby networks that benefit from preservation drives, each commitment reaffirms our obligation to safeguarding the regular and social legacy of our planet for people in the future to appreciate.

Fundamentally, adding to protection endeavors is an excursion of stewardship and obligation, where each move we make as voyagers has the ability to shape the fate of our planet. By upholding the security of normal and social legacy locales, supporting feasible travel industry rehearsals, and advancing ecological mindfulness and schooling, we can guarantee that our movements abandon a tradition of preservation and maintainability—aa demonstration of our obligation to save the magnificence and trustworthiness of the Earth for a long time into the future.

9

Chapter 9: Reflecting on Transformative Experiences

Understanding the Force of Movement to Change Points of View and Points of View

Understanding the force of movement to change points of view is essential for valuing the significant effect that vivid encounters can have on our self-improvement and advancement. Travel, with its capacity to open us to new societies, scenes, and lifestyles, has the momentous ability to challenge our assumptions, expand our perspectives, and reshape the focal point through which we view the world.

The charm of understanding this extraordinary power lies in the acknowledgment that movement isn't simply about ticking off objections on a list of must-dos or gathering visa stamps; rather, it is an excursion of self-revelation and edification—aa journey into the obscure that holds the possibility to transform us in manners both unpretentious and significant. Whether it's seeing the greatness of nature in a distant wild, drenching ourselves in the dynamic rhythms of a clamoring city, or associating with individuals whose lives and points of view vary immeasurably from our own, heading out opens ways to new encounters and bits of knowledge that have the ability to change us at the most profound levels.

However, understanding the force of movement to change points of view isn't just about the objections we visit or the encounters we have enroute; it's additionally about the excursion internal—the course of self-reflection and contemplation that movement definitely rouses. As we explore through new scenes and explore social contrasts, we are compelled to face our own predispositions, suspicions, and constraints, provoking us to reexamine our convictions, values, and needs considering new encounters and viewpoints.

Besides, understanding the force of movement to change points of view offers an opportunity to develop a more prominent feeling of sympathy, empathy, and interconnectedness with our general surroundings. As we submerge ourselves in the lives and accounts of individuals from different foundations and societies, we start to see ourselves reflected in the essences of outsiders, perceiving the normal mankind that ties us together and rises above geological and social limits.

Be that as it may, maybe the best award for understanding the force of movement to change points of view lies in the potential chance to become specialists of positive change on the planet. Whether it's supporting civil rights and natural protection, advancing diverse comprehension and discourse, or essentially living all the more carefully and purposefully in our day-to-day routines, the groundbreaking encounters we gain through head-out rouse us to be more humane, gallant, and connected with residents of the world.

Basically, understanding the force of movement to change points of view is an excursion of enlivening and edification, where each experience turns into a chance for development and self-revelation. By embracing the groundbreaking capability of movement with an open heart and a receptive outlook, we can leave on a journey of investigation and self-acknowledgment that drives us to new skylines of figuring out, compassion, and satisfaction—both inside ourselves and in our general surroundings.

Thinking about Self-improvement and Advancement Acquired Through Movement Encounters

Considering self-awareness and improvement acquired through movement encounters is a critical part of the excursion, offering an opportunity to stop, introspect, and value the significant ways in which our experiences have formed us as people. Whether it's venturing beyond our usual ranges of familiarity, defeating difficulties, or embracing new points of view and approaches to being, travel has an extraordinary capacity to catalyze individual change and encourage a more profound comprehension of ourselves and our general surroundings.

The appeal of pondering self-awareness and improvement lies in the valuable chance to perceive the manners by which travel has extended us past our apparent constraints and impelled us towards self-disclosure and self-acknowledgment. From the thrilling highs of summiting a moving top to the peaceful snapshots of thoughtfulness while watching a dusk into the great beyond, each movement experience makes a permanent imprint on our spirits, engraving recollections and examples that shape the course of our lives in significant and unforeseen ways.

However, considering self-awareness and advancement isn't just about praising our victories and triumphs; it's likewise about embracing the illustrations gained from our disappointments and mishaps enroute. Whether it's wrestling with pining to go home in an unfamiliar land, exploring social errors, or facing the uneasiness of venturing into the obscure, making a trip provokes us to defy our feelings of dread, frailties, and weaknesses head-on, cultivating flexibility, mental fortitude, and confidence all the while.

Besides, considering self-awareness and improvement offers an opportunity to develop a more profound feeling of appreciation for the actual excursion—the individuals we've met, the spots we've seen, and the encounters we've shared enroute. As we think back on our movements and point of view, we start to see the strings of interconnectedness and synchronicity that wind through the embroidery of our lives, uncovering the excellence and intricacy of human involvement with all its extravagance and variety.

However, maybe the best reward for thinking about self-awareness and advancement lies in the feeling of strengthening and mindfulness that comes from realizing that we are the draftsmen of our own predetermination. Whether it's graphing another course throughout everyday life, seeking after our interests with recharged energy, or basically embracing the excursion with an open heart and a receptive outlook, travel advises us that the best experience of everything is the one that exists in—the excursion of self-revelation and self-acknowledgment that drives us to the most genuine and most valid articulation of ourselves.

Basically, considering self-awareness and improvement is an excursion of self-revelation and strengthening, where each experience turns into a venturing stone on the way to more prominent grasping, empathy, and satisfaction. By embracing the examples gained from our movements with appreciation and modesty, we can tackle the extraordinary force of the excursion and turn out to be stronger, more fearless, and more alive to the endless conceivable outcomes that look for us out and about ahead.

Investigating the Manners by which Travel Difficulties Suspicions and Encourage Compassion

Investigating the manners by which travel difficulties raise suspicions and encourage compassion is a significant part of the excursion, offering an extraordinary focal point through which we can see the world and our place inside it. As we adventure into new regions and draw in with different societies and viewpoints, travel has a momentous capacity to destroy generalizations, widen how we might interpret humankind, and develop sympathy and empathy for other people.

The appeal of investigating how travel difficulties suppose and cultivate sympathy lies in the amazing chance to break free from the limits of our own social, social, and philosophical air pockets and step into the shoes of others with an open heart and a receptive outlook. Whether it's seeing firsthand the versatility of networks living in the result of cataclysmic events or participating in discussions with local people whose educational encounters vary tremendously from our own, venture out welcomes us to challenge our assumptions and embrace the intricacies and subtleties of human involvement with all its variety.

In any case, investigating how travel difficulties suppose and encourage compassion isn't just about widening our points of view; it's likewise about perceiving the interconnectedness of mankind and our common humanity that ties us together across topographical and social partitions. As we drench ourselves in the lives and accounts of individuals from various different backgrounds, we start to see ourselves reflected in their battles, expectations, and dreams, manufacturing associations that rise above language, identity, and nationality.

Besides, investigating how travel difficulties supposing and encouraging sympathy offers an opportunity to develop a more profound feeling of compassion and empathy for other people, as well as respect for ourselves. As we take the stand concerning the victories and hardships of those we meet enroute, we come to understand that we are not really unique all things considered—that underneath the surface distinctions of language, culture, and appearance, we as a whole offer similar essential cravings for affection, association, and having a place.

Yet, maybe the best compensation for investigating how travel difficulties presuppose and cultivate sympathy lies in the change that happens inside ourselves—the enlivening of our souls and brains to the excellence and intricacy of the world and our place inside it. Whether it's figuring out how to see the world through new eyes or finding a freshly discovered feeling of sympathy and understanding for the people who walk in various directions, travel turns into an impetus for self-awareness and social change that stretches out a long way past the limits of our singular processes.

Basically, investigating how travel difficulties challenge presumptions and cultivate compassion is an excursion of self-disclosure and illumination, where each experience turns into a chance for development and change. By embracing the examples gained from our movements with lowliness and interest, we can turn out to be more humane, more compassionate, and more associated residents of the world—crossing over isolates, building spans, and making a more splendid and more comprehensive future for all.

Perceiving the Worth of Thoughtfulness and Self-Disclosure While Out and About

Perceiving the worth of thoughtfulness and self-disclosure while out and about is a fundamental part of the movement experience, offering a significant chance for self-awareness and internal change. As we venture through new scenes and explore the intricacies of social trade, travel gives a rich ground to self-reflection, contemplation, and the investigation of our most profound longings, fears, and goals.

The appeal of perceiving the worth of reflection and self-disclosure lies in the valuable chance to strip back the layers of our own personalities and reveal the insights that lie underneath. Whether it's tracking down comfort in the tranquility of nature, journaling about our encounters, or taking part in reflection and care rehearsals, travel makes space for us to associate with our deepest selves, acquiring understanding of our convictions, values, and inspirations all the while.

Yet, perceiving the worth of reflection and self-revelation isn't just about searching internally; it's likewise about embracing the excursion as a mirror for our own development and advancement. As we experience new difficulties and explore new territory, we are compelled to stand up to our own limits and uncertainties, provoking us to develop versatility, boldness, and confidence, notwithstanding misfortune.

Besides, perceiving the worth of reflection and self-revelation offers an opportunity to develop a more profound sense of identity, mindfulness, and credibility in our lives. As we gain lucidity about what our identity is and the main thing to us, we are enabled to live more purposefully, pursuing decisions that line up with our qualities and desires, as opposed to being driven by outer assumptions or cultural tensions.

In any case, maybe the best award for perceiving the worth of reflection and self-revelation lies in the feeling of strengthening and satisfaction that comes from knowing ourselves profoundly and legitimately. Whether it's acquiring clarity about our life reason, tracking down the boldness to seek after our interests, or just embracing the excursion with an open heart and a receptive outlook, travel turns into an impetus for self-improvement and change that reaches out a long way past the limits of our singular processes.

Generally, perceiving the worth of reflection and self-revelation is an excursion of self-disclosure and strengthening, where each second turns into a chance for development and internal change. By embracing the excursion with interest and transparency, we can open the maximum capacity of our movements to stir our hearts and psyches to the magnificence and marvel of the world and our place inside it.

Embracing the Extraordinary Capability of Movement to Motivate Positive Change in Oneself and the World

Embracing the extraordinary capability of movement to rouse positive change in oneself and the world is the climax of the excursion—an acknowledgment of the significant effect that our encounters out and about can have on our day-to-day routines and the existences of others. As we think about the examples we took in, the development experienced, and the associations made, we are emboldened to outfit the insight acquired from our movements and channel it into significant commitments that elevate and enable both ourselves and the people around us.

The appeal of embracing the groundbreaking capability of movement lies in the acknowledgment that our undertakings are not just about gathering encounters or collecting recollections; they are tied in with catalyzing self-awareness and cultural change, about becoming specialists of change and diplomats of empathy, understanding, and trust. Whether it's pushing for civil rights and ecological preservation, chipping in with grassroots associations, or just living all the more carefully and purposefully in our regular routines, making a trip motivates us to be the change we wish to find on the planet.

However, embracing the groundbreaking capability of movement isn't just about having an effect on the planet; it's likewise about respecting the actual excursion—the ups and downs, the delights and distresses, the snapshots of stunningness and pondering that have formed us into the individuals we are today. As we embrace the extraordinary force of movement, we come to see our undertakings not as simple capers but rather as sacrosanct journeys—an excursion of the spirit that leads us home to ourselves, to our most genuine and true selves.

Besides, embracing the groundbreaking capability of movement offers an opportunity to develop a more profound feeling of association and having a place on the planet. As we perceive our interconnectedness with all creatures and the actual planet, we are called to act with sympathy, compassion, and graciousness towards ourselves, towards others, and towards the Earth, perceiving that we are inseparably connected in the snare of life.

However, maybe the best prize for embracing the groundbreaking capability of movement lies in the feeling of direction and satisfaction that comes from realizing that our processes definitely affect the world. Whether it's abandoning a tradition of benevolence and sympathy, motivating others to leave on their own excursions of self-revelation and change, or just living with a more noteworthy feeling of euphoria, appreciation, and presence, travel turns into an impetus for individual and aggregate development that stretches out a long way past the limits of our singular lives.

Generally, embracing the extraordinary capability of movement is an excursion of enlivening and strengthening, where each step turns into a demonstration of the force of the human soul and the limitless conceivable outcomes that exist in every one of us. By embracing the insight acquired from our movements with modesty and appreciation, we can become reference points of light and problem solvers in a world that is eager for mending, association, and change.

10

Chapter 10: Continuing the Adventure

Arranging Future Ventures and Defining New Objectives and Yearnings

Arranging future ventures and defining new objectives and yearnings denotes the start of a thrilling section in the excursion of experience, offering an opportunity to imagine the conceivable outcomes that lie ahead and chart a course for new encounters and disclosures. As we ponder the recollections made and examples gained from our past movements, we are enlivened to dream greater, reach further, and set out on new undertakings that push the limits of our usual ranges of familiarity and grow our viewpoints.

The appeal of arranging future voyages and defining new objectives and yearnings lies in the expectation of the obscure—the adventure of envisioning the spots we'll go, the individuals we'll meet, and the encounters we'll have enroute. Whether it's investigating far-off wild regions, submerging ourselves in energetic social celebrations, or leaving on legendary excursions of self-disclosure, the conceivable outcomes are unfathomable, restricted exclusively by our creative mind and eagerness to embrace the unexplored world.

However, arranging future voyages and laying out new objectives and yearnings isn't just about the objections we'll visit or the encounters we'll have; it's additionally about the actual excursion—the method involved with dreaming, arranging, and planning for the experiences that lie ahead. From investigating likely objections and making head-out schedules to setting aside cash and making strategic courses of action, the excursion starts some time before we set foot on unfamiliar soil, and each step enroute turns into a chance for development and self-disclosure.

Besides, arranging future ventures and putting forth new objectives and yearnings offers an opportunity to develop a sense of direction and course in our lives. As we put our focus on new skylines and seek after our interests with restored energy, we are helped to remember the force of movement to motivate us, challenge us, and change us into our best selves. Whether it's learning another dialect, dominating another expertise, or overcoming a long-held dread, travel turns into an impetus for self-improvement and self-satisfaction that stretches out a long way past the limits of our singular processes.

Yet, maybe the best prize for arranging future ventures and defining new objectives and yearnings lies in the feeling of fervor and probability that comes from realizing that the best undertakings are on the way. Whether it's the excitement of venturing into the obscure or the delight of reconnecting with natural places and faces, each new excursion turns into a chance for disclosure, development, and association—an opportunity to compose the following section in the narrative of our lives, each experience in turn.

Fundamentally, arranging future voyages and laying out new objectives and desires is an excursion of expectation and fervor, where each fantasy turns into a venturing stone on the way to a day-to-day existence loaded with importance, reason, and satisfaction. By embracing the potential outcomes that lie ahead with energy and assurance, we can change our fantasies into the real world and make a future that is essentially as rich and energetic as the experiences we envision.

Incorporating Examples Gained from Previous Encounters into Day-to-Day Existence

Coordinating examples gained from previous encounters into our day-to-day existence is a significant part of the excursion of experience, offering an opportunity to gather intelligence and bits of knowledge from our movements and apply them to our day-to-day schedules and cooperations. As we consider the recollections made and the difficulties that survive, we are helped to remember the versatility, mental fortitude, and flexibility that exist in us, motivating us to move toward every day with restored reason, appreciation, and deliberateness.

The appeal of incorporating examples gained from previous encounters into our day-to-day existence lies in the acknowledgment that movement isn't just about the spots we go to or the things we see; it's likewise about the illustrations we learn and the development we experience enroute. Whether it's developing a feeling of flexibility notwithstanding difficulty, embracing the magnificence of temporariness and change, or figuring out how to explore a new landscape with effortlessness and modesty, the insight acquired from our movements turns into a directing light that enlightens our way ahead, illuminates our decisions, and forms our points of view in significant and surprising ways.

In any case, integrating examples gained from previous encounters into daily existence isn't just about applying viable information or abilities obtained out and about; additionally, it's about exemplifying the qualities and standards that lie at the core of the movement experience—values like interest, sympathy, and social getting it. Whether it's coming difficulties with a receptive outlook and a feeling of experience or stretching out consideration and sympathy to those we meet enroute, the illustrations gained from our movements become a diagram for carrying on with a daily existence loaded up with importance, reason, and association.

Besides, incorporating illustrations gained from previous encounters into our regular day-to-day existence offers an opportunity to develop a more profound sense of presence and care in our everyday schedules. As we pay attention to our viewpoints, sentiments, and activities, we start to see the excellence and miracle of the world from a new perspective, enjoying each experience as though it were a valuable gift to be treasured and relished.

In any case, maybe the best compensation for integrating examples gained from previous encounters into regular day-to-day existence lies in the feeling of strengthening and satisfaction that comes from realizing that our movements definitely affect what our identity is and the way in which we appear on the planet. Whether it's the certainty acquired from venturing beyond our usual ranges of familiarity, the compassion developed from strolling in the shoes of others, or the appreciation motivated by the excellence and variety of the world, each illustration learned turns into a signal of light that guides us on our excursion of self-revelation and development.

Fundamentally, integrating illustrations gained from previous encounters into regular daily existence is an excursion of mix and exemplification, where each experience turns into an educator and each second turns into a chance for development and change. By embracing the insight acquired from our movements with lowliness and appreciation, we can make a daily existence that is wealthy in significance, reason, and satisfaction—aa daily existence that mirrors the excellence and marvel of the world we've investigated and the illustrations we've advanced enroute.

Supporting a Feeling of Interest and Investigation in Ordinary Schedules

Sustaining a feeling of interest and investigation in regular schedules is a major part of carrying on with a daily existence loaded up with amazement, revelation, and probability. As we progress from the fervor of movement to the commonality of home, we are welcome to develop a mentality of receptiveness and receptivity, embracing every second as a chance for experience and development, paying little mind to where we track down ourselves.

The charm of supporting a feeling of interest and investigation in regular schedules lies in the acknowledgment that life is an excursion of constant revelation—an embroidery woven from the strings of our encounters, collaborations, and perceptions. Whether it's taking an alternate course to work, attempting another recipe for supper, or starting up a discussion with a more unusual person, our daily existence gives us endless chances to investigate our general surroundings and grow our viewpoints in unforeseen and significant ways.

Yet, supporting a feeling of interest and investigation isn't just about searching out new encounters or pushing the limits of our usual ranges of familiarity; it's likewise about developing a feeling of miracle and wonderment in the standard snapshots of life. Whether it's wondering about the excellence of a dusk, tracking down delight in the giggling of kids, or valuing the basic joys of a hot cup of tea on a virus winter's day, regular daily existence turns into a material whereupon we can paint the shades of our fantasies and desires, imbuing every second with importance and reason.

Besides, supporting a feeling of interest and investigation in ordinary schedules offers an opportunity to extend our association with ourselves, other people, and our general surroundings. As we approach every day with a feeling of miracle and interest, we become more present, more drawn in, and more alive to the boundless conceivable outcomes that exist in and around us, encouraging further associations and more extravagant encounters all the while.

However, maybe the best prize for supporting a feeling of interest and investigation in regular schedules lies in the feeling of satisfaction and happiness that comes from carrying on with a daily existence lined up with our most profound interests and values. Whether it's the excitement of finding a novel or new thing, the fulfillment of conquering a test, or the harmony that comes from embracing the current second with great enthusiasm, day-to-day existence turns into an excursion of delight, disclosure, and self-acknowledgment—an excursion worth enjoying and commending constantly.

Fundamentally, supporting a feeling of interest and investigation in ordinary schedules is an excursion of enlivening and strengthening, where each second turns into a chance for development and change. By moving toward every day with an open heart and a receptive outlook, we can develop a daily existence loaded up with amazement, interest, and plausibility—aa daily existence that mirrors the excellence and lavishness of the world we possess and the endless possibility that exists in every one of us.

Looking for open doors for development and experience in natural environmental elements

Looking for open doors for development and experience in natural environmental elements is a demonstration of the unfathomable potential for revelation and change that exists inside our regular daily existences. While movement frequently summons pictures of outlandish objections and distantness, truly, the world is abounding with valuable open doors for investigation and development, even in the most common of spots.

The charm of looking for valuable open doors for development and experience in recognizable environmental elements lies in the acknowledgment that experience isn't simply an objective; it's a mentality—an approach to moving toward the world with interest, boldness, and a feeling of receptiveness. Whether it's exploring one more climbing trail in our local park, taking an unconstrained excursion to a nearby town, or drenching ourselves in another culture while voyaging abroad, the excitement of finding the obscure and pushing our limits keeps us alive and locked in. By searching out these valuable open doors for development and learning, we extend our viewpoints as well as develop how we might interpret ourselves and our general surroundings. Eventually, it's about the objections we reach, however, the excursion we take to arrive.

www.ingramcontent.com/pod-product-compliance
Lightning Source LLC
Chambersburg PA
CBHW030457010526
44118CB00011B/974